'Mission from "the rest" to "
features of church life in Euro
mission raises are many ar
practical experience and wel
this work an invaluable tool
practice.'

Rev Dr Martin Robinson, Principal of ForMission College, Author

Mission and Movement

A Study of Ethiopian and Eritrean Evangelical Churches in the UK

Hirpo Kumbi

instant
ap□stle

First published in Great Britain in 2018

Instant Apostle
The Barn
1 Watford House Lane
Watford
Herts
WD17 1BJ

British Library Cataloguing-in-Publication Data

A catalogue record for this book is available from the British Library

This book and all other Instant Apostle books are available from Instant Apostle:

Website: www.instantapostle.com

E-mail: info@instantapostle.com

ISBN 978-1-909728-89-9

Printed in Great Britain

Dedication

I dedicate this book to the first pioneers of Ethiopian and Eritreans Fellowship in the UK: Kassaye and Maureen Degefu, Dr Berhanu Habte, Dr Milkias Shambo, Yohannis Gizaw, Dr Abraham Araya, Lia Mehari, Margaret and Ergate Ayana. Also, I express my deep gratitude to Ergate, who provided me with evidential documents and gave me an accurate account of this ministry's start in the UK.

I would also like to dedicate this book to Pastor Abera and Beletu Habte, who started the first Amharic TV ministry, El Shaddai TV Network.

Acknowledgments

I am grateful to Dr Richard Whitehouse who encouraged me in this research and for contributing a foreword.

Also, my appreciation and thanks go to Dr Clement Katulushi and David Judson, from whom I have received much support during the process.

Finally, I wish to express my deepest thanks to Dr Martin Robinson for his commendation.

Contents

Foreword

Like the Greek god Janus, this work faces two ways. First, it addresses the presence of one set of diaspora African churches in the UK and then, by implication, raises the issue of the missional relationship between these churches and the indigenous evangelical churches of the host nation. On the way, it discusses pertinent issues surrounding the interface between Church and culture and how that affects the practice of mission. Although he doesn't use the terminology in this piece of research, my friend Hirpo Kumbi is an example of what has been called 'reverse mission'. That is a convert who is, at least indirectly, the product of mission activity originating from UK shores and who has now become a missionary to this country. The former missionary-sending nations have now become recipients of a wave of missionaries from countries formerly considered to be 'the mission field'. However, that vocabulary has become redundant as in the light of Scripture and a cooler look at history we have at long last recognised that mission is no longer the privilege or the burden of the West. We now realise that mission is 'from anywhere to everywhere'.

Hirpo is a dedicated missionary to our culture who has taken on British citizenship so as to become more effective in furthering his calling to this country, and I have been privileged to work with him over the past ten years, both among diaspora Ethiopian churches and indigenous churches in the UK. We have worked to help the diaspora churches as they seek to embrace their calling as missionaries to the host culture. In the early stages of our collaboration, Hirpo embarked on this piece of research investigating UK-based diaspora churches from his homeland. The intention was to gain insight into the way these churches establish themselves and go on to relate to the host culture. In the event, this piece of research has proved helpful in formulating a missional strategy for the future.

There is a growing body of literature relating to so-called 'reverse mission' in general, but a dearth of detailed case studies focusing on particular groups. This work goes some way to filling that gap and it is our hope that it will spark off a series of studies concentrating on other groups. As this study suggests, not all diaspora churches focus on mission to the wider culture as they prefer outreach to their own ethnic or cultural milieu. Nevertheless, increasing numbers of expatriate churches express a desire to evangelise the host culture and many of them become frustrated at the lack of progress in doing so. This work tentatively points the way to solutions as it explores the relationship between cultures and the gospel and calls for collaborative structures that will enable more effective partnerships for missional engagement between host culture and diaspora culture churches.

One of the intriguing aspects of *Mission and Movement* is the way it sets the establishment of Ethiopian diaspora churches in the UK in the context of their historical and political background back at home and the way that recent developments there affect the thinking and structures of these churches in a present-day European setting. The sometimes simplistic 'reverse mission' terminology begins to open up in light of the intricate relationships between mission, colonialism and gospel heritages that creates a distinctive Church culture which, when transplanted on to the foreign soil of contemporary Britain is forced to adapt once more if is not to become merely a dying means of home culture preservation. Kumbi asks some difficult questions as he explores these issues through field work and in-depth interviews that throw up some puzzlement and uncertainty on the part of some Ethiopian church leaders. This impasse has resurfaced frequently in our joint work since this research was conducted as we and ForMission College have worked with diaspora churches from Ethiopian and other ethnic and cultural backgrounds. The sheer variety and forms of diaspora church plants – Brazilian, Colombian, South African, Korean, Asian, Iranian and Chinese to name but a few – suggests that more concentrated studies like this one will enhance our understanding of multicultural missional movements and enhance our ability to 'win the West' for Christ.

One of the spin-offs from this study could be the emergence of a determined and thoughtful collaborative strategy designed to equip diaspora church leaders to be more effective in their stated aim of reaching the host culture with the message of the gospel for the twenty-first century. Crucial to this undertaking might be a clear-headed understanding of what vital values and characteristics these churches and their leaders would bring to the revitalisation of the British Church. Moreover, such collaboration could lead to the emergence of a new generation of culturally savvy leaders on both sides of the divide whose contribution to missionary development would be invaluable.

As Hirpo concludes his study:

> As missional movements, the Ethiopian and Eritrean Christian churches in the United Kingdom see themselves as Jesus' ambassadors and witnesses of His love. When stripped of the divisive political and individualistic elements which beset the churches occasionally, the key contribution Ethiopian and Eritrean churches can make to both their own communities and British society is the embodiment of a loving and caring gospel whose invitation transcends national boundaries.

It is hoped that as you read on, you will be challenged and inspired to pick up the baton in this ongoing relay as we learn from them.

Dr Richard Whitehouse

Introduction

This book began life as research material for my dissertation submitted as part of the Springdale College MA in missional leadership course validated by the University of Wales.[1] My purpose in embarking on these life-changing studies was to equip myself to become a more effective missionary to European culture where God sent me as he spoke to me while I was pursuing my leadership responsibility at Ethiopia Emmanuel United Church in Arsi Negele town, and this calling has been recognised and I have since been apostolically commissioned for this purpose by the Fellowship of Churches of Christ in Great Britain and Ireland.

It might be worthwhile to share a few biographical details that will serve to highlight my journey as a missionary to the UK and point to some pertinent issues that affect most African (and other) diaspora church movements working in the European context, especially those with an ambition to reach the host cultures with the gospel. The MA course, which was part of my preparation as a so-called 'reverse missionary', threw up many issues that I had not previously considered. Some of these considerations were underlined and confirmed by the

---

[1] Springdale College has since been reformulated and rebranded as ForMission College, of which I am currently Chief Operating Officer.

piece of research that forms the bulk of this book. The motive for publishing them is to enable fellow workers in this field to benefit from discoveries – and some mistakes – that I have made. In the process, it is hoped that the multicultural missional church movement will be enhanced and accelerated as it contributes to the revitalisation of the Church and the advancement of the kingdom of God in this country.

My vision on first arriving in this country at the end of 2002 was to work as an evangelist and church planter. Since I had a limited command of the English language I began by focusing on my own people group. I found that by hanging around at bus and train stations in large centres of population it was relatively easy to recognise people from the Horn of Africa from their distinctive features. I also knew that whatever their language, I could make myself understood. My initial approach was to welcome new Eritrean and Ethiopian asylum seekers to my home and offer them friendship. I would also attend any kind of community event where there was a chance to gather with other people from my own background and offer familiar food, language and customs designed to make them feel less isolated. As an ambitious and entrepreneurial church planter, I was able to establish small congregations in Leeds, Sheffield, Bradford and London and to support other church plants in Newcastle. Some of these grew and flourished, but I came to recognise that I was spreading myself too thinly and that none of them proved successful in reaching the host communities, which was my long-term goal.

In the early days in Leeds I worshipped with an indigenous Baptist church in the hope of forming a multicultural partnership. This did not prove to be possible, although I formed a close friendship with Andrew Hinds, an assistant pastor in the congregation at the time. His friendship and encouragement helped develop my thinking in terms of the benefits of cross-cultural interaction. As part of my desire to better understand the UK scene and to learn how to approach mission in the host community, I enrolled on the MA course in missional leadership and it was there that my ideas broadened. This research report was an integral part of that process.

Among other things, I came to see that the best way forward was twofold: first, to form a relationship with an indigenous church body open to inter-cultural cooperation; second, to promote mission through training. Both of these aims began to be realised through my relationship with Dr Martin Robinson, the principal of Springdale College, later to become ForMission College, and other college teachers including Dan Yarnell, the national coordinator of the Fellowship of Churches of Christ in Great Britain and Ireland, and Dr Richard Whitehouse, who also mentored me. Their encouragement inspired me to begin a learning centre in Leeds which was to become the North Campus of ForMission College, of which I became director. This all followed from the 'Multiply' local leaders' course, developed in conjunction with Dr Whitehouse to equip the leaders from our Ethiopian church plant in Leeds to work more effectively in the multicultural context of the UK. This course was later extended nationally and has been attended by emerging indigenous church leaders, as well as those from other ethnic groups including Colombians, Ghanaians and Eritreans.

All of this may seem a long way from planting diaspora churches – or even from working as a church planter myself – but I have learned by example that slower is sometimes faster, and that developing other leaders is in the long run a more effective means of extending one's reach. In particular, this research and the developments that flowed from it have convinced me that there are common themes relevant not only for leaders within the Ethiopian and Eritrean churches, but also for all leading immigrant congregations and any indigenous British leaders working with them.

It may be too late for some congregations to change direction because their cultural mindset is fixed, and it would be harder work changing the orientation of the bulk of their older members, whose attitudes are deeply entrenched in maintaining their own culture and their sense of personal identity. This is particularly true for those who did not come to this country with the intention of planting churches but merely wished to find a congenial arena to maintain their faith. The main benefits of these findings may be for younger, more flexible congregations and intentional reverse missionaries. Nevertheless, even culturally rooted traditional congregations may be able to see that their forms of worship and church structures are only likely to survive two generations at the most. But, given sufficient vision, such congregations could sponsor more flexible missional offshoots.

As things stand, many diaspora churches in the UK display common themes reflected in this research that are likely to lead to long-term failure, but which can be turned around. The desire to retain patterns learned from the home culture are likely to bring stagnation and eventual cultural isolation resulting in congregational death. If these churches are to survive, they need to go beyond preserving cultural norms or even continually evangelising a shrinking cultural population. However, in the light of the themes explored here, and subsequent experiences growing out of it, progress can be made. One dominant theme is that the second generation of immigrant families will be lost unless accommodation is made to the fact that English will be the preferred language of communication for many of them. Even traditional culture congregations are aware of this, but what is easily missed is that characteristics such as simplicity of living and passion for the gospel are the most important part of their Christian cultural heritage that could make them the most effective evangelists of their peer groups in the host culture.[2]

At the present time, there are few signs of these lessons being learned. In the Ethiopian/Eritrean congregations there are indications that power struggles and church splits dominate the horizon because there is a passion for ministry without great understanding of the priority of mission – the prime reason for any church's existence, whatever its cultural background. Ministerial ability so easily leads to pride of position rather than fulfilling the calling to reduplicate missional leadership. The young

---

[2] I deal with these issues in more detail my book *The Culturally Intelligent Leader* (Watford: Instant Apostle, 2017).

leaders of tomorrow long to reach their cross-cultural peers.

The first Ethiopian church in London planted another over a decade ago as part of its growth. Since this research, this second church has separated, declaring itself independent. In addition, a group of ministers has split away from this first church and started another fellowship; again, a group of young adults from this founding church left and started a new ministry. All these splits happened because of the founding church's adherence to an irrelevant church leadership culture. This tendency towards church splits doesn't only happen in London, but also other cities, including Birmingham and Leeds. However, the Emmanuel Christian Fellowship in Leeds and the Leeds Christian Fellowship have merged and are now named Maranatha Evangelical Church of Leeds. This is an encouraging start towards unity among churches.

In the main, Ethiopian/Eritrean churches do not seem to have an effective strategy for producing tomorrow's church, let alone for reaching the host culture. So far, to my knowledge there are no indigenous converts in these churches, nor are there many indications of indigenous missionaries working with them to bring about change. However, there are ripples on the surface; some of our students have picked up on these themes and are beginning to work for change. One group of young mentee Ethiopians in their early twenties who are fluent second-generation English speakers have formed an evangelistic team in London working among their peers and the younger diaspora generation, as well as indigenous youngsters, and another one is starting in Manchester. This creates hope for the formation of a multicultural outward-looking church fully committed to mission. Rhema Faith Church, an Eritrean and Ethiopian congregation in Birmingham led by Pastor Rehoboth Beyenne has an American missionary couple working with them to develop an English-speaking worship congregation for younger church members as a step towards forming a multicultural expression of church enabling the younger generation to reach out cross-culturally to their peers. These are straws in the wind; what we need is a full-blown gale of change, and it is my hope that this book will at least be a starting point, a catalyst for revolutionary adjustment.

Chapter One

Understanding Ethiopia and Eritrea

In this chapter, the main focus is to provide a brief outline of the book, as well as to provide an explanation of the motivation for undertaking this piece of research. Chapter Two is concerned with a literature review and provides insight into Ethiopian Christianity as well as diaspora and mission. The research methodology and findings make up chapters Three and Four. From chapters Five through to Seven, thematic discussions are presented, drawing on the research findings and showing how the research question has been resolved. Chapter Eight helps bring the various threads of the research together with recommendations and a conclusion. However, as will be shown later, the research is as much a personal discovery as it is a scholarly study of mission from the Ethiopian and Eritrean perspective. Later in this chapter, I will provide a brief history of Ethiopia in general, and Ethiopians and Eritreans in Britain in particular. However, it is necessary to start with a brief understanding of the key concepts used in the research question. These include what it means to be a missional church, and culture and mission.

Missional

According to Stetzer,[3] the word 'missional' means doing mission right where you are, that is, adopting the posture of a missionary, and learning and adapting to the culture around you while remaining in line with the Bible. Doing mission is being intentional and deliberate about reaching others for Christ.[4] In the case of Ethiopian and Eritrean churches in the UK, mission is about engaging in a planned and thought-out undertaking to proclaim Jesus. Missional does not seek to reach a people in a distant far-away land but begins to work through the immediate culture and with the local people. Culture is to do with the environments, practices or traditions that shape how we interpret our world.[5] Chapter Five explores the concept of culture in more detail. Suffice to say the influence of Ethiopian culture on Christianity is of as much interest as is the influence of Christianity on Ethiopian culture, especially in the light of questions around identity for the emerging generation of Ethiopians in the UK.

Early history

References to Ethiopia may be found in the Bible, indicating that it is a country with a history which stretches back to antiquity. Walls narrates the long history of Ethiopian Christianity beginning from Axum and the reign of King Ezana and then spreading over huge areas 'by

---

[3] See bibliography for full details of sources of quotes.
[4] Stetzer, 2006, p19.
[5] Roxburgh and Romanuk, 2006, p23.

processes we still do not fully understand'.[6] Between 1855 and 1974, Ethiopia witnessed events that culminated in the emergence of a centralised modern bureaucratic state.[7] Adejumobi gives an outline of the events around the occupation of Ethiopia, from 1889 when Italy considered Ethiopia as one of its protectorates to 1895 when Italian forces invaded Ethiopia.[8] The influence of the Church even then was explicit in Menelik's proclamation rejecting Italian protection:

> Enemies have now come upon us to ruin the country and to change our religion ... Our enemies have begun the affair by advancing and digging into the country like moles. With the help of God I will not deliver up my country to them ... Today, you who are strong, give me of your strength, and you who are weak, help me by prayer.[9]

The following year, Ethiopians emerge victors at the Battle of Adwa and Italy is forced to recognise Ethiopian independence although it still maintains control of Eritrea. In 1935, Italy invaded Ethiopia again, this time capturing Addis Ababa and causing Emperor Haile Selassie to flee into exile. According to Aren, the invaders expelled even the foreign missionaries, causing church development to stall.

---

[6] Walls, 2002, p88.
[7] Adejumobi, 2007, p22.
[8] Adejumobi, 2007, pxvii.
[9] Adejumobi, 2007, p29.

Haile Selassie was able to address the League of Nations assembly challenging the Italian invasion. In 1941, Ethiopia, with the help of British and Commonwealth soldiers, defeated Italy and Haile Selassie reclaimed his throne. When the war was over, much of Ethiopia was in disrepair and 'the faith of many had been tried. But God called forth people from different parts of the country' to keep the gospel alive.[10]

Recent history

Ethiopia

During the 1990s, Ethiopia was under the presidency of Mengistu Haile Mariam who had taken over from Emperor Haile Selassie in a bloody coup d'état. Growing up in Ethiopia as a young man was for me and my peers a period of anxiety and tension due to ongoing wars being waged between different social groups. Renewed armed hostilities between Ethiopia and Eritrea stemmed from an earlier history prior to my birth, but then the countries existed as one country until 1992. There were attempts by groups such as the Oromo[11] who sought their own independency from the rest. The fighting caused many people from Oromo society and other minority groups to flee to other parts of the world, including the United Kingdom. This research in part is a narrative of those people who left Ethiopia and Eritrea for various reasons, including fleeing from wars, who are now living in the UK,

---

[10] Aren, 1978, p533.

[11] This author comes from the Oromo and draws on personal experience too. See also Chapter Three findings.

and have established mission in community anew. This chapter gives a short history of Ethiopia as well as a personal experience of that history, combining a personal and national narrative leading in the following chapters to the Ethiopian and Eritrean Christian narrative.

The effects of the migration can be traced through the establishment of churches of Ethiopian origins based on mother tongues including Oromo. Thus, a salient characteristic of Ethiopian and Eritrean churches around the world is the prevalence of languages such as Amharic and Tigrigna. In the UK, the Oromo language is used in no more than three churches, despite the fact that there is a fairly large number of Oromo people from Ethiopia living in the UK. This has been noticeable in my role as a leader of a particular community and has in part influenced my interest in mission and church planting. In a way, it seems that these ethnic-specific churches are developing as a means to native language preservation, although it is possible to see them as vehicles of evangelism to other ethnic groups. In a much broader sense, my experiences with Ethiopian and Eritrean churches have led me to explore whether emerging churches from other cultures[12] in the UK can become a missional movement that reaches out to the host culture.

To define Ethiopia is not an easy thing. The task is fraught with difficulties so perhaps it is wiser to attempt a description than a definition. Bonk (1984) is courageous enough to attempt a definition, saying the term Ethiopia comes from two Greek words meaning 'to burn' and 'face', and hence rendering a literal meaning 'land of burnt

---

[12] Central Intelligence Agency, 2012.

faces'.[13] This definition is regarded as offensive by many Ethiopians who do not define themselves by physical impression, pointing out that for example a great many Ethiopians are tall, but basing their identity on physical stature does not honour their being. Even the term 'Black Africans' to describe Ethiopians does not do justice to understanding Ethiopia at all. Hence a wiser approach perhaps is to invite the reader to an engagement with the living history of Ethiopia and Eritrea. Furthermore, it is important to note that the Oromo diaspora rejects the term 'Ethiopia' for whom the term conjures colonialism and repression. Owing to this, being Ethiopian is not part of Oromo self-identity.[14] Collyer and de Guerre (2006) explain how a group of Oromo and Amhara refugees in Brighton and Hove were split by politics – the Oromo members of the group rejected the term 'Ethiopia' and formed an Oromo Society, which the Amhara members were welcome to join but did not.[15] There is yet another use of the term 'Ethiopia', adopted by some to signify black freedom and independent nationhood, seen as a legacy of Ethiopian culture.[16]

Geographically the countries are in the Horn of Africa or East Africa. Until recent history, Ethiopia and Eritrea used to exist as one country. Despite this, some Eritreans claim that Eritrea was an originally an independent country. Ethiopia, covering an area of 1,106,000 sq km, has a population close to 90,873,739 while Eritrea has a

---

[13] Bonk, 1984, p ix; also Adejumobi, 2007, p2.
[14] Fransen and Kuschminder, 2009, p21.
[15] Fransen and Kuschminder, 2009, p21.
[16] Adejumobi, 2007, p2.

population of 5,939,484.[17] Projections are that Ethiopia will have a population growth to 115,382,091 by 2025.[18] In Ethiopia, the religious landscape based on the 2007 shows a breakdown into Orthodox 43.5 per cent, Muslim 33.9 per cent, Protestant 18.6 per cent, traditional 2.6 per cent, Catholic 0.7 per cent, other 0.7 per cent.[19] Overall, about 65.02 per cent of the population are Christian.[20]

Eritrea

Pateman (1990) in *Eritrea: Even the Stones Are Burning* presents a version of history in which the Eritrean narrative is unique and different from that of Ethiopia. He argues against the view that the two countries share a common history, tradition and mythology and attempts to show how over the decades Eritrea has fought off its would-be colonisers, distant (Italy and Britain) and close (Ethiopia). He argues that the Ethiopia–Eritrea one nation unity was forged in problems. In 1950 Britain and the United Nations determined on a federation of two disparate bedfellows – Ethiopia and Eritrea. It seems, however, that a majority of Eritreans were opposed to this move. Ethiopia also accepted federation under protest – it wanted unconditional union with Eritrea.[21] From this

---

[17] Johnstone and Mandryk, 2001, p243; see also https://www.cia.gov/library/publications/the-worldfactbook/geos/et.html (accessed 19th January 2018).

[18] Johnstone and Mandryk, 2001, p243.

[19] https://www.cia.gov/library/publications/the-world-factbook/geos/et.html (accessed 5th February 2018).

[20] Johnstone and Mandryk, 2001, p244.

[21] Pateman, 1990, p6.

account, it can be deduced that prior to 1950 when it formed the federation with Ethiopia, Eritrea charted its own course in history until 1960 when it was annexed by Ethiopia. In terms of religion, there existed in Eritrea a plurality of religions identifiable by language. Referring to Southern Ethiopia, Aren refers to Islamic envoys who could not speak Arabic apart from the salutation and creed.[22]

Pateman claims that 93 per cent of Tigrigna speakers were Christian and 7 per cent Muslim.[23] Aren traces the relationship between evangelical Christians in Ethiopia and Eritrea further back to 1927 when a number of Eritreans joined the Mekane Yesus Church, and even earlier when some Oromo evangelists visited Eritrea around 1910.[24] The story of the two countries continues to intertwine even in the UK today.

Ethiopian and Eritrean churches in the UK today

When considering the history of the Ethiopian and Eritrean churches in Britain, a key factor to note is that the Church started off as one Church in line with the one nation known as Ethiopia. Following the independence or secession of Eritrea from Ethiopia in 1992, the Church in the United Kingdom also split into two strands along the lines of the home nations. This is illustrated in 1996 with the naming

---

[22] Aren, 1999, p368.
[23] Pateman, 1990, p5. There is detailed information here about the religious composition in various parts of Eritrea.
[24] Aren, 1999, pp85, 231.

of churches such as Bethel Eritrean Church and Ethiopian Christian Fellowship of Great Britain. However, with the establishment and rise of new and emergent churches, the churches felt little need for the use of nationally identifiable names, arguing that the Church did not belong to a specific nation but to Christ, and that both Ethiopians and Eritreans are called to serve God irrespective of their cultural grounds. Another prevailing view held by some churches was that the shared history and culture was too strong to lead to separate churches, despite the political boundaries already drawn. It must be borne in mind that the development of evangelical churches from the Horn of Africa shares strong semblances, and even in some cases the same origins. However, here a word of clarification is necessary. During the course of the research, it was evident that a section of the community did not regard itself as Ethiopian, and here reference is made to the Oromo people.[25] A respondent church self-described themselves as distinct from, and not a part of Ethiopia. Without any undue disrespect to any community involved, the current conventional terms of 'Ethiopia' or 'Eritrea' have been used. This does not in any way endorse any political position of any group, except to acknowledge the sensitivities present in these labels and identities.

On the whole, this belief in a united Christian faith, and despite any secessionist issues arising from the Eritrean and Ethiopian split, the Ethiopian and Eritrean communities based in the United Kingdom do not seem to

---

[25] A Home Office guidance identifies the existence of movements in the UK which seek a separate Oromo state. This insight into Oromo comes from the writer's own knowledge of the community concerned.

harbour the divisions inherited from their home countries. Thus, it is common to see both Ethiopian and Eritrean people meeting together as one church. In situations like this, as has been experienced in Leeds, Birmingham and some churches in London, Amharic is the medium or language of the worship service. This has also to do with the fact that Ethiopians are the majority, especially in those churches holding their services in Amharic. However, there is a separate Eritrean church in Leeds whose services are held in Tigrigna. This is in addition to the fact that a number of Eritreans worship together with Ethiopians in Amharic services.

Chapter Two

Mission and Migration

In order to provide an overview of the body of evidence influencing this research, Chapter Two plays a fundamental role, highlighting and reviewing literature on the subject. This chapter not only gives an overview of the broader subject of the African Christian diaspora, more pertinently, it gives an insight into the Ethiopian and Eritrean Christian churches in Britain.

Ethiopia is one of the world's top tourist destinations, given its rich history, heritage and close access to the pyramids. However, Ethiopian and Eritrean communities living abroad may be seen as remote, and there is a dearth of literature about diaspora Ethiopians and about Ethiopian and Eritrean churches in particular. Despite the paucity of literature on evangelical Ethiopian and Eritrean churches in the UK in particular, and in Africa in general, a few texts on Ethiopia exist which address the subject of the Christian narrative, its historical development and direction. Foremost among these are the works of Gustav Aren, whose prolific works have contributed much to Ethiopian church studies.

Pioneers

Aren's *Evangelical Pioneers in Ethiopia: Origins of the Evangelical Church Mekane Yesus* provides a critical account of the development of Christianity in Ethiopia addressing the tensions, challenges and achievements of the early evangelical pioneers. It is from the works of Aren that much can be learned about the lives of missional pioneers such as Onesimus Nesib and Gundima Tusmus. Not only does Aren introduce us to Christian history, but perhaps to the real story of Ethiopian Christian thought could be discerned in some of his works. Aren's *Envoys of the Gospel in Ethiopia* presents a solid account of a historical understanding of Christianity in Ethiopia. The striking thing about *Envoys of the Gospel in Ethiopia* is the depth of knowledge and understanding of the subject matter. In this book, the breadth of thought is as vast as the people of whom the book gives account. The name of Aleqa Taye may not be familiar to many people and yet it is his legacy that *Envoys of the Gospel in Ethiopia* documents and honours. The teachings of Taye point to a way of life that permeates present day Ethiopian Christianity: that the core of Christian living is in seeking, it is to 'find out what pleases the Lord', and by so saying urging a habitual delving into the Scriptures.[26] Hence if today's Ethiopian Christian mission is to be described succinctly, it is a sacred enterprise born of a renewal of Christian living and based on the teachings of the Bible. Mission is therefore witnessing.

---

[26] Aren, 1999, p58.

Aren was professor of theology at Uppsala University, prior to which he served as field director at the Swedish Evangelical Mission in Ethiopia, and was a founder and first principal of the Mekane Yesus Seminary. He was one of the architects of the Ethiopian Evangelical Christian Mekane Yesus (EECMY). His readership includes renowned scholars such as Bengt Sundkler and John Bauer.[27]

Aren not only provides an interesting historical account but also presents Ethiopian models of bedrocks of faith, such as Onesimus Nesib and Aleqa Taye, for anyone seeking to emulate the life of Jesus. In a chapter about various early Ethiopian evangelists, Aren offers a deeper insight into what Ethiopian mission entails. This is in an account about the Boji mission. Boji is described as the cradle of the Mekane Yesus Church,[28] a church whose reach into the present day touches even some of those who now live in the United Kingdom, and have in their own rights set about planting churches of their own. Boji is the place where the missional work of pioneers such as Aleqa Taye met with the beginning work of Gebre-Ewostatoes Ze-Mikael in order to reach out to the Oromo people.[29] Boji, being the cradle of Mekane Yesus Church, by implication is the first mission church in Ethiopia. Not only did it seek to proclaim the gospel to the Oromo, but also to win over the large Muslim population. An achievement of the

---

[27] Aren, 1999, p5.

[28] According to its website, the church has 5,279,822 baptised and 2,465,637 communicant members making it the largest Lutheran Church in Africa.

[29] Aren, 1999, pp60-61.

Mekane Yesus Church is the first translation of the Bible into Oromiffaa. An understanding of the development of the evangelical Church of Eritrea is given the same thorough and sensitive depth as is the history of the Ethiopian Mekane Yesus Church. The works of Gustav Aren are therefore essential for gaining information about the evangelical Church in both Ethiopia and Eritrea.

The origins of Bethel Church, which has now spread across the UK, can be traced to Mekane Yesus Church, and to some leaders in the UK such as Ergate Ayana. Furthermore, from Aren's work, it is evident that Christian mission to the Oromo and Eritrea has its roots at Boji. It is also evident that for today's evangelical harvest, the seed was planted in the mid-1890s. The sense of purpose is evident in Ethiopian Christianity; the gospel is too precious to lose so it can only be preserved by carrying it and proclaiming it in places where it has never been taken. That Christian living meant more than food and drink for these pioneers is shown in accounts of how at times these missionaries had to face fear and danger in mission. However, the early Ethiopian Christians, after being forced by the Italian chaplain to give up their church building, reunited as a community and pooled their few resources in order to build a church.[30]

Migration

According to Haar (1998), there were close to 48,839 Ethiopians and thirty-eight Eritreans in Europe in 1994, while the numbers of Ethiopians travelling to the United

---

[30] Aren, 1999, p509.

States more than doubled and were second only to Nigerians. As Haar has observed, intercontinental travel from Africa happens because African migrants leave their homes to build a new life. Among the reasons for this is political persecution or religious conflict. A book which delves more broadly into Africans living overseas is Gerrie ter Haar's book, *Halfway to Paradise: African Christians in Europe*. The book deals with the rather wider scope of Africans in Europe, and could be seen as a diversion from the more particular interest in Ethiopian and Eritrean churches. Although the book does not offer any statistics for Ethiopian and Eritrean people in the UK, it offers important material in understanding the environment in which Ethiopian and Eritrean churches operate, and the concept of African-led churches in the United Kingdom.

Strangers and Sojourners: Religious Communities in The Diaspora edited by Gerrie ter Haar (1998) is a useful contribution to the understanding of the issues of African-led churches and their communities in as far as two chapters in this book are concerned with the subject. A chapter by Kalilombe, 'Black Christianity in Britain',[31] laments the lack of literature around the subject. This aside, Kalilombe (1998) traces black Christianity in terms of African and African-Caribbean migrants. The African immigrants he refers to are those from West Africa. Tracing their arrival in the early 1950s, the majority of African immigrants came as students to acquire the education and formation required for leadership in their newly independent nations. The levels of and reasons for African immigration today are greater than at that time, especially

---

[31] Kalilombe, 1998, pp173-194.

considering that some parts of Africa suffer political turmoil. However, the issues around cultural identity, Christian mission and growth are still pertinent. Kalilombe observes that for the many Africans now permanent residents in Britain, their children who have been born and raised in Britain have no real cultural links with their parents' original homelands. Britain is their home. Despite this assertion, and true to the understanding that Christians are a pilgrim people, on a dual nationality of God's kingdom and their earthly residence, efforts by African-led churches sometimes include embedded cultural elements in keeping with the original homelands. Hence it is the case that within the Ethiopian and Eritrean churches, prayer and worship services are held in both English and Amharic, serving to illustrate the community's dual citizenship credentials.

Another chapter in *Strangers and Sojourners* worth mentioning is the article by Haar (1998), 'The African diaspora in Europe: some important themes and issues'.[32] It points out that one of the most disturbing aspects of present-day migration policy in Europe is its tendency towards the exclusion of black people. In Britain, the siege mentality is hyped by some newspapers and migration watch groups and translated into political rhetoric such as 'Secure Borders', a part of the UK Border Agency's logo strapline. Populist political immigration schemes tend to further segregation despite the piecemeal attempts at community cohesion undertaken by some community organisations and charities. However, Haar's article grapples with a range of issues, from even the concept of

---

[32] Haar, 1998, pp37-58.

'diaspora' tracing its roots to Jewish experience of exile and life outside Judea, to cross-cultural harmony among communities. This is useful in that it provides an understanding of the burden of being and the responsibility of relationships.

In terms of mission, it places a challenge to the walls of segregation which lead to exclusive comfort zones, stating that mission demands 'going forth' and that mission involves every person. In this sense therefore, Haar rightly sees the call of African Christianity as a necessary invitation for Europe to revisit its relations with non-Western believers. Haar states that empirical evidence suggests that it is not a perceived fundamentalist minority which seeks to demarcate itself from the Christian majority, it is often the latter who wish to demarcate themselves from the former by claiming to be different. Moreover, this can be viewed, for the purposes of this book, that it is not the intention of Ethiopian and Eritrean churches to alienate themselves through advocacy of a cultural preservation, but rather an effort to reach out to the United Kingdom with a gospel which births itself through inter-cultural engagement.

Chapter Three

Researching the Church in the UK

In this chapter, I cover the research methodology and offer a theoretical discussion informing the research process. I also describe the research methods used in collecting or finding information. The research used the ethnographical technique based on the anthropological approach.

Definition

The ethnographical technique allows the researcher to become one of the cultural participants, offering insights into how the world is seen, and how he engages with it.[33] According to Baszanger and Dodier, in using the ethnographical approach by definition, the researcher is present in two agencies: as data gatherer and as a person involved in activities directed towards other objectives.[34] A longer definition of ethnography is as follows:

> The study of people in naturally occurring settings or fields by methods of data collection which capture their social meanings and

---

-194.

an, 2008, p410.

[34] Baszanger and Dodier, 2004, p12.

ordinary activities, involving the researcher participating directly in the setting, if not also the activities, in order to collect data in a systematic manner but without meaning imposed on them externally.[35]

I was keen to gather information from Ethiopian and Eritrean churches where I have close contacts directly and indirectly. However, as in the definition above, I was an active participant as an insider, sharing with the participants a common language and a common religious experience, as well as common values and traditions. The information was intended to resolve whether or not the churches were merely serving an ethnic specific agenda or a broader inclusive mission. The desire to ensure authentic experiences were obtained and accurately understood made the ethnographical approach highly suitable. I chose the questionnaire method because I was aware that ethnographic approach relies mainly on participant observation and key participant interviewing. Thus questionnaires were useful in understanding participants within the context of cultural preservation or cross-cultural engagement to complement interviews held with key participants in order to get an in-depth understanding of the development of Ethiopian and Eritrean churches. This fits with the comment by Miller and Glassner (2004) that

> those of us who aim to understand and document other's understandings choose qualitative

---

[35] Bell, 2005, p16.

interviewing because it provides us with a means for exploring our research subjects, while granting these points of view the culturally honoured status of reality.[36]

All the methods used in the research, whether interviews, discussions or questionnaires, worked together through participant observation to enable me 'as far as possible, to share the same experiences as the subjects, to understand better why they act in the way they do and "to see things as those involved see things"'.[37] Given the fact that I came as an 'insider' into the research, it has not been difficult to achieve acceptance by individuals and groups from the Ethiopian and Eritrean churches.

Furthermore, the reason for using interview techniques was so as to obtain information, thereby leading to the findings in the next chapter. Holstein and Gubrium (2004) observe that 'interviewing provides a way of generating empirical data about the social world by asking people to talk about their lives'.[38]

I occasionally use narrative to explain certain elements of the research. The ethnographical technique is also appropriate in handling other narratives, those Ethiopian and Eritrean accounts of mission in the UK which are also in cross-cultural dialogue. Although a certain level of statistics has been given, the purpose is not to underline a diversion to the quantitative research, but rather to

---

[36] Miller and Glassner, 2004, p127.

[37] Bell, 2005, p17.

[38] Holstein and Gubrium, 2004, p140.

develop a sense of the Ethiopian and Eritrean UK communities as part of mission.

Insider and outsider perspective

From the onset, this work has been concerned with the development of Ethiopian and Eritrean churches in the UK. Part of the motivation behind this research is my personal experience, as a native Ethiopian now resident in the UK. The purpose of this research in part is to provide an understanding of Ethiopian and Eritrean engagement with mission. As a practising minister of religion, I offer inevitably more of an 'insider' than an 'outsider' perspective. This is not to suggest that the outsider perspective is lacking in this research, but rather to underline the author's shared identity with the research question and possession of cultural knowledge. Temple and Moran (2006) show the manner in which a perspective such as the insider perspective could enhance research, especially among migrant communities. In my case, access to respondents was made possible mainly because our shared identity of culture, faith and language helped foster communication and overcome the language barriers that would potentially exist in a cross-cultural setting. Here it is necessary to remember that several languages, in addition to English, are spoken across the Ethiopian and Eritrean communities in the United Kingdom. Furthermore, these communities exist in a contentious political historical background still pertinent even in present times.

Library research included the use of both print and non-print media, a scrutiny of church documents and also the use of academic literature. A critical tool in the research methods has been the use of the University of Leeds library. Reading around the subject proved a challenge, mainly because, as observed earlier, there is a dearth of books in this discipline. For example, an electronic search of the university library's full catalogue revealed only two texts dealing with Ethiopian churches. When this was enlarged to extend to Ethiopian communities in the UK and or Ethiopian and Eritrean churches in the UK, the search found 32,000 references, and trawling through this list only exposed about ten titles with some relevance. It proved very challenging to find a body of literature covering Ethiopian and Eritrean communities in the United Kingdom in university libraries in Leeds or further afield. The closest to any semblance of reference to Ethiopian and Eritrean churches in the United Kingdom was *Art That Heals: Image as Medicine in Ethiopia,* [39] and *African Ark: Peoples of the Horn.* [40] This seems to indicate a greater scholarly interest in Ethiopians living in Ethiopia than in Ethiopians in the diaspora.

In addition to written sources, I also consulted more widely with experts in the field of theology and religious studies. I met Dr Kevin Ward, a University of Leeds expert in African Christianity and religions with whom I spoke about the research question. He was able to reassure me that my work covered a field or discipline which suffered

---

[39] Jacques Mercier (London: Prestel, 1997).
[40] Carol Beckwith with Angela Fisher (London: The Harvill Press, 1990).

from a paucity of scholarly material and research. [41] Another contact was Dr Amare Desta, a lecturer at Southbank University and a leading member of an Ethiopian think-tank in London who offered helpful insights into the history of Ethiopia.

Face-to-face interviews

As has been implied, part of the research method has included the use of face-to-face discussions in order to develop a clearer understanding of the issues facing Ethiopian and Eritrean communities in the UK, and to develop a more accurate narrative around the work of mission by Ethiopian and Eritrean churches in the UK. Besides discussions with scholarly experts, a number of face-to-face discussions were held with indigenous Ethiopian and Eritrean church leaders resident in the United Kingdom, both established and emergent. Dr Yoseph Mengistu, a lecturer at the School of Oriental and African Studies in London, was a research contributor through this method.[42] Based at SOAS, Dr Mengistu is well placed to understand issues facing Ethiopian and Eritrean churches in the United Kingdom and this was evident in telephone conversations held with him and in subsequent face-to-face discussions. Dr Mengistu is also an Ethiopian church leader, one of the early ministers involved in

---

[41] Discussion held with Dr Kevin Ward on 2nd February 2012 at the Department of Theology and Religious Studies, Hopewell House, University of Leeds, Leeds.

[42] Initial telephone discussion was held on 2nd February 2012 followed by a weekend meeting in London.

church planting who is both an academic and a practitioner. In terms of the research, therefore, there was much gained from telephone conversations and face-to-face discussions held with experts and lay respondents and selected respondents in order to build knowledge and insight into developments in Ethiopian and Eritrean churches and mission in the United Kingdom, and to be able to envisage the shape of Ethiopian and Eritrean inter-cultural penetration to promote the gospel. In part, therefore, although there is a dearth of published materials, this research will hopefully contribute to filling the gap.

By face-to-face discussions, what is meant in this research is discussions around the research topic held in person with selected respondents. The use of face-to-face discussions as a research method is commonly used in qualitative research and effectively complements other methods, such as research questionnaires, interviews or focus groups. Face-to-face discussions help establish rapport with respondents leading to a solicitation of in-depth thinking on a particular issue or topic. They exploit more fully the expertise, experience or knowledge of the research participant. In this case, face-to-face discussions were held in various settings meant to offer ease and convenience to participants. For example, some discussions were held in university campus locations while others were held in offices or coffee shops or in private residences. It was important to create a feeling of trust, confidence and security in the process in order for the research itself to be authentic.

As further conversations developed it became helpful to seek other means of conducting face-to-face discussions without resorting to costly journeys from Leeds to London and elsewhere. The use of Skype, an online internet-based programme, enabled real-time live video conferencing to happen. This therefore gives a slight variation to what is meant by face-to-face meeting, dialogue or conversation.

For the purpose of this research, I travelled to London and had discussions with a number of people, paying visits to three churches, namely the Ethiopian Christian Fellowship, Bethel Eritrean Church, and Kebron Eritrean Church.[43] Between them, there were approximately 850 people attending services on a Sunday in Amharic and Tigrigna. From observations that Sunday, the Tigrigna and Amharic services were mainly attended by either Ethiopian or Eritrean community members. There was no visible indication of people from the host community or other nationalities. However, the Ethiopian Christian Fellowship also held an English service attended mainly by children and young people.

Face-to-face discussions fall under the interview method. Interview techniques may embrace the methods already mentioned above, such as telephone, email, Skype or face-to-face discussions. The reason interviews or face-to-face discussions were undertaken is that they are an effective tool in dealing with life histories. In this case, the research question can only be fully met by the personal narratives of various Ethiopians and Eritreans. Furthermore, the research method used took advantage of

---

[43] The author travelled to London from 18th February 2012 to 20th February 2012.

the rapport existing between the author and respondents, a relationship based on trust.

Data collection

The sample selection was based on my own contacts and the contacts of pastors from their congregations. The sample comprised pioneer church leaders and pastors and church members. A questionnaire that was non-sponsored and unsolicited was sent to 300 members of Ethiopian and Eritrean churches. Questionnaires were sent by email while some were issued by hand with responses being collected immediately after completion and some responses sent back by post. The churches involved represented a cross-section of established Ethiopian and Eritrean churches across the United Kingdom. Twenty-seven questionnaires were sent to selected church leaders in various cities. These leaders were selected on the basis that they exercised leadership for a majority Ethiopian and Eritrean congregation, or in some cases were considered leaders of emergent Ethiopian and Eritrean churches in the United Kingdom. To ensure anonymity, no personally identifiable information of questionnaire respondents has been used. All respondents were asked to respond to questions related to church activity, specifically cultural, pastoral and missional experiences, thus limiting the statistical analysis contained in this book. Table 1 (Chapter Four and Appendix A Part B) gives an overview of their responses.

The experience I gained in the use of modern methods of communication, especially in terms of information and computing technology, has also led to a reinterpretation of mission. Research methods involved the use of smartphones, landlines, computers and even mail through the post. Social networking based around computer or internet-based features such as Skype and Google+ are fairly recent trends, but older technologies such as television still have a place, but with the added platform of internet TV or online broadcasts, podcasts and similar. These tools may play a great role in many emergent Christian churches.

One of the consequences of the use of modern methods of technology is that the concept of cultural preservation, whether real and effective or imagined and ineffectual, is that the church engaged in mission sees the whole world as a mission field. A television programme may be designed for a greater and broader audience beyond the immediate sphere of the minister. Once on air, a television, radio or internet programme is not shackled by culture. Hence a small house church may have a global outreach because of its online activity.

While reading round the subject involved access to university libraries and then taking advantage of a variety of books, journals and even electronic material, a few unexpected documents came into my possession. These were the original copy of the minutes of the initial meetings held to establish the Fellowship of Ethiopian Christians in the United Kingdom, and also the governing document of the Fellowship. In addition, I was sent a recently written but yet unpublished memoir by Mr and Mrs Kassaye Degefu of Preston. These sources helped provide insight into the motivations driving the Ethiopian pioneering church leaders and the beginnings of revival in Ethiopian

Christian mission in the United Kingdom. The research also scrutinised governance documents for the Emmanuel Christian Fellowship, an Ethiopian-led church in Leeds. I have strong links with this church, being part of the pastoral team there.

Chapter Four

Analysing the Churches

In this chapter, I will describe the responses received from a variety of methods used, including questionnaires, discussions, interviews and the use of primary resources. Based on the research findings, this chapter also aims to establish an understanding of the notion of community for Ethiopians and Eritreans in the United Kingdom, and how this sense of community impacts on mission.

The book will consider these responses under a number of themes and their salience in regard to the questionnaire sample. The findings will be given with reference to whether or not Ethiopian and Eritrean churches exist to preserve culture or as missional movements. In order to do so, some responses from the respondents have been reproduced here. In all cases, the extracts are reproduced verbatim and therefore, in some cases, there are spelling or grammatical mistakes originally written by respondents.

Even the very process of soliciting questionnaire responses had moments of difficulty. In one case, a questionnaire was sent to a church leader who sent this reply:

I quicly [sic] went through your questionnaire, but it is mainly designed for _____ churches. Is there another questionnaire designed for _____ Church? Sorry I don't have information on _____ churches.[44]

The truth of the matter is that the respondent saw his community as under the bondage of Ethiopia and that their identity was not Ethiopian. This shows how much of the cultural and political issues and difficulties need to be kept in perspective. Here the question becomes more pertinent – are Christian churches from Ethiopia and Eritrea cultural dead ends or instruments for cross-cultural missional penetration? The strong likelihood is that churches established with a strong ethnic foundation will perpetuate a mono-cultural growth continuum. Such churches will either grow or stagnate depending on political developments linked to their home nations instead of spiritual maturity. The following analysis both highlights the difficulties of the process and tests this thesis.

---

[44] The blank spaces have been inserted to preserve the respondent's anonymity.

Table 1: Collated Results of Responses to Questionnaire from Church Members

Issue	Answers					Total (263)
1 – Faith	EE	UK	OC	NYC		
	182 (69%)	52 (18%)	27 (10%)	1 (0.3%)		262
2 – Friendship	0	1-2	3-5	6-10	11+	
	24 (9%)	19 (7.2%)	26 (10%)	40 (15%)	104 (36%)	213
3 – British enquiry	Yes	No				
	148 (56.3%)	111 (42.2%)				259
4 – Witnessing	Yes	No				
	115 (44%)	143 (54.4%)				258
5 – Barriers	Language	Not Welcome	Reserved	Other		
	115 (44%)	57 (22%)	21 (8%)	67 (25.5%)		260
6 – Culture	Yes	No	Don't Know			
	156 (59.3%)	48 (18.3%)	51 (19.4%)			255
7 – Social action	Yes	No	Don't Know			
	205 (78%)	23 (9%)	33 (13%)			261
8 – Crossing culture	Yes	No	Don't Know			
	77 (29.3%)	127 (48.3%)	55 (21%)			259

Key to Table 1

EE – Became a Christian in Ethiopia or Eritrea

UK – Became a Christian in United Kingdom

OC – Became a Christian in another country other than United Kingdom, Ethiopia or Eritrea

NYC – Not yet a Christian

From the table, we can interpret the data thematically. The following analysis considers the data drawn from the questionnaire responses and examines this in the light of information provided by church pastors.

Faith

From the responses concerning faith, a majority of respondents, 69 per cent, indicated that they became Christians in their native Ethiopia and Eritrea. Only 18 per cent became Christians in Britain, while only 0.3 per cent of the respondents had not yet become a Christian although they were attending church services. The data shows Ethiopian and Eritrean churches reaching out to witness to their own communities. None of those who became Christians are indigenous British which indicates the need for more missionally effective engagement.

Interaction with host culture

Regarding interaction between Ethiopian and Eritrean Christians and British people, there were a variety of responses. There are about 9 per cent Eritreans and Ethiopians who have no social or friendship contact with British people, while over 36 per cent enjoyed individual friendships with more than eleven British friends. However, it seems this friendship does not necessarily translate into gospel outreach when it is considered that there are no indigenous British brought to Christ by the churches and that church membership is made up entirely of Ethiopian and Eritrean people. From this response, we can develop some understanding about relationships within the mission context and the feasibility of cross-cultural penetration.

Evangelism

A key element of mission is the ability of every Christian to witness to Christ, through their lifestyles and also in being able to share the gospel; 56.3 per cent discuss the gospel while 42 per cent do not share gospel with others. The problems, shown by other data in this table, are the barriers in the way Ethiopian and Eritrean Christians interact with their British hosts. Furthermore, sharing the gospel does not seem to result into tangible British converts.

Barriers to faith sharing

In the research questionnaire, responses to barriers experienced by church members in communicating their faith drew on their experiences with their British neighbours, friends and the general public; 44 per cent of the respondents felt that a lack of fluency in English on their part was a barrier to sharing the gospel with non-Ethiopians and Eritrean communities, while 22 per cent felt that British or non-Ethiopians and Eritreans were not friendly or approachable enough to enable a discussion about their faith. Only 8 per cent saw their individual personalities – that is, being shy or having a reserved manner – as a barrier to sharing their faith with members of other communities; 25.5 per cent chose the broader 'other' category as barriers. Under this other, it was only from later verbal discussions that difficulties such as lack of cooperation and unity among Christian churches were explained as barriers to spreading the gospel. The problem of language was also mentioned by some pastors with some saying 'Language barrier which we are trying tackle', and 'We have little commandment of the English language'.[45]

These two comments echoed the view of most of the church members and leaders, that there was a problem of communication to which a solution might be found in community cohesion initiatives, mainstream services and other schemes, but clearly this is a concern for effective cross-cultural missional penetration. The attendant problem with a poor command of English is that opportunities for engaging with non-Ethiopian and Eritrean communities are not taken up and instead churches concentrate mainly on their own communities as mission field.

Social action

Seventy-eight per cent of respondents were of the view that Ethiopian and Eritrean churches were making a positive contribution towards life in the community as opposed to

---

[45] Pastors in questionnaire responses.

23 per cent who disagreed; 33 per cent of the respondents were not aware of the social action their churches were undertaking. In terms of the overall responses this 78 per cent was the highest score and suggests that social action is a significant part of church mission. However, lack of awareness of this as an evangelistic tool by members may explain why indigenous British people do not come to Ethiopian and Eritrean churches. Considering this aspect, there is some correlation with some church newsletters and reports showing how churches engage with the communities in the provision of various services. More importantly, the churches don't just see themselves as being about prayer and worship but believe that mission is about proclaiming a risen Jesus who is concerned with the totality of a person's life. For one respondent, social action is embedded in Scripture[46] which provides a framework of the church's agenda. The 611 Centre is a scheme for reaching out to migrants and destitute people as a direct application of Scripture. It is similar to a drop-in community centre where community members, the homeless and other vulnerable people can go and be provided with some support. This is part of the missional role of this church:

> In our church we do evangelise for all people regardless of their ethnic and nationality. However the ethnic minorities seem to be more approachable and accessible as they have a need

---

[46] Isaiah 61:1 is the text used and is identified as the 611 Centre providing practical help.

of immigration problem and the church organise open door programs.[47]

However, social action on the part of the churches is also about helping Ethiopians and Eritreans in the United Kingdom to understand their identity in a new culture, and providing space for culture to speak to culture. This idea is developed further in Chapter Five. Unfortunately, 13 per cent of Ethiopian and Eritrean Christians do not seem to be aware of the missional outreach of their churches.

Cultural preservation

Findings show that 59.3 per cent were of the view that the churches play a significant role in preserving Ethiopian/Eritrean culture, as compared to 18 per cent who do not link cultural preservation to the church. The result of this question is affected by the fact that 19.4 per cent do not know what the church is doing along cultural lines. These statistics are not surprising bearing in mind that most church services are held in Amharic and Tigrigna. It is puzzling however that 19.4 per cent are not aware whether or not their churches have a cultural inclination.

It is also necessary not to generalise because some of the responses indicated deliberate efforts to engage with the British public and non-Ethiopian and Eritrean communities. For example, one response saw secularisation as the barrier to mission saying:

---

[47] Pastor D H in questionnaire response.

> Secularisation is working widely among them. In
> some instances they show a willingness to hear
> the good news and yet they are highly influenced
> by their day-to-day life concern.[48]

This response presents the case that mission is faced by a greater challenge: a modern technologically dependent world in which Christianity may seem to have little to contribute.

Cross-cultural mission

The largest number of respondents, 48.3 per cent, were of the view that Ethiopian and Eritrean churches were not doing enough to witness Christ outside of their immediate ethnic communities. This rather high figure showing dissatisfaction with outreach activities is not made any lighter by the 21 per cent of respondents who were ignorant of activities undertaken by churches to engage with the host community or non-Ethiopian and Eritrean people. The churches' cross-cultural engagement activity does not seem effective and correlates with the initial findings that only 18 per cent came to faith in the UK. It may be inferred here that on the one hand Ethiopian and Eritrean churches are inward-focused, only comfortable to engage through social action, or share the gospel with members of their own communities, and that on the other hand they are clearly finding it difficult to undertake cross-cultural penetration for mission. The response from the

---

[48] Pastor I in questionnaire response.

general church membership fits with comments made by some church leaders, some of whom were of the view that:

> In some churches I think I can say yes, in the bigger cities for the first generation it is OK to promote the culture. Hence, I'm not convinced and I have great concern for the second generation as they have a language and culture barrier.[49]

Another simply said, 'Yes, there are some cultural influence.'[50]

The insight gained from these responses is that Ethiopian and Eritrean churches are seen as having a function in culture preservation. This is no different from other churches that operate in any cultural setting. However, the point is that as the new generation of Ethiopian and Eritrean Christians assume leadership from the old leaders, they begin to engage with a set of values and a mindset which may be radically different from that promoted or addressed by the pioneer church planters. Through this new leadership, the churches are now beginning to put into place strategies intended to embrace the new culture by introducing English services. Of the various responses received from the pastors, a majority confirmed this strategy, reporting some regular English services for young people and spaced or monthly English services for the older members.

---

[49] Pastor S M in questionnaire response.
[50] Pastor O K in questionnaire response.

Church leaders

In terms of findings from the responses submitted by pastors, this book has alluded to certain aspects of how their views confirm or contradict the views of the general membership. A key finding regarding this has been around the schemes or strategies designed to engage in cross-cultural activities. Here the focus of activity has been the use of English in worship and praise services. According to one pastor, their plan is 'To extend our horizons to non-Eritrean/Ethiopian people, that's why we have a Bible study that conducted 100% in English'.[51] However, there was a much deeper finding regarding strategies for cross-cultural penetration which were not explicit or codified but seen as the practice of embracing the host culture. So it is not just about the use of English in church services but also the adoption of a new lifestyle, as seen in attitudes towards fashion and clothing, food and social etiquette. However, it was acknowledged in discussions that there were cultural differences which still needed negotiating, that cross-cultural engagement did not mean a shedding of the Ethiopian/Eritrean identity to assume the new British one. This is a point made by a church leader when he said:

> The Church will first need to examine itself and agree on a common ground with regard to cultural issues, eg secular music. There are a number of cultural issues that need to be retained within the community, I do not believe the Church has yet reached this stage as it is trying to

---

[51] Pastor A G in questionnaire response.

work on a common ground in particular with the challenges presented with the second generation.[52]

In the response above, there is an indication that the churches are moving towards some common framework or ground in thinking ahead about the shape of things to come for the church. Here, mission also begins to become important. Cross-cultural penetration becomes an issue of necessity to avoid becoming a cultural dead end. However, in order to go beyond seemingly impossible challenges, the framework for greater and wider appreciation of the urgency of mission could provide a means to emphasise the overarching command of Jesus and the Scriptures to go and make disciples.

Such a framework and the formation of a common ground also addresses the problem of unity, a factor which was implied in various interviews and questionnaire responses but brought out more sharply in this response:

> They should work together, respecting each other, accepting each other and supporting one to another. More of that they should show love for other sister churches and they should be role model for their congregation. We should break the barrier of the language and should get involve in the British culture and create a communications.[53]

---

[52] Pastor G S M in questionnaire response.

[53] Pastor A G in questionnaire response.

The expectation in the response above is that Christians are all one family, and that they should be united in love and in mission as one family. The writer thus laments the apparent divisions among the churches, seeing these as distracting from scriptural authority. It is a barbed remark on churches which concentrate more on mono-cultural existence instead of cross-cultural growth.

A point of attention for these churches too is the question of a younger generation who may be distanced from partisan or nationalistic politics which may be of great importance to the older generation. Young people may not regard 'bondage' or identity in the same light as older people, and yet there is the strong possibility that churches with a strong passion for ethnic culture might nurture new churches to promote mono-cultural ministry. It seems to be the case that balancing ethnic home culture as represented by the older generation with the host British culture as represented by the new generation is something most churches are already thinking through. According to one respondent:

> The churches main mission is to reach people with the gospel and the church has done this as evidenced by the growth within the different Eritrean and Ethiopian churches … One of the other aims and purposes … is to ensure that the Eritrean community retain its culture while also gating to now [sic] the British culture and make contribution.

On the one hand, mission is about the gospel. On the other, the gospel is expressed in culture just as culture is built in the church.[54] According to Stetzer, the missional church is always looking for the best way to reach the culture it lives in at that point in time.[55] The missional church delights in the culture(s) of its members while also embracing the culture of its new circumstances. Social action is seen as part of mission. The direction the churches take is about achieving the purposes for which they have been established.

It is in view of the resilience of church planters that even the initial tensions which existed in the mid-1980s – and may still exist today – were faced. In tracing the development of the first Ethiopian and Eritrean churches, starting with the 1974 birth pangs in Preston and moving onto the 1984 London phase, revival was not a popular desire. Even then, there was a lack of support for other church planting in London itself. A respondent pioneer active in that period recalls:

> My big barriers was from the church planted before I came to London. It was full of religious and cultural mind. Due to that, it had been very difficult to talk about faith. Because of that I have been passed through in many difficult situations.[56]

It seems that in the experience of this respondent, the failure in new church planting was because of a traditional mindset framed in the Christendom image. The birth of the first Ethiopian church in London was not

---

[54] Stetzer, 2006, p21; Walls, 2004, p68.

[55] Stetzer, 2006, p23.

[56] Pastor A G in questionnaire response.

received as a signal to spur on rapid growth, instead, the new church seemed to be seen as meeting the need for mission, an end in itself and not a means. And yet it seems that quite the opposite happened in the rest of the UK, which saw a multiplication of Ethiopian and Eritrean churches across the nation.

Another issue raised in the various responses received concerns resources. Ethiopians and Eritreans called out to plant churches in the UK do not often enjoy the patronage of a benefactor in their country of origin. Owing to this, church planting may begin without any independent or back-up finance. Emmanuel Christian Fellowship was established with the costs for venues, hospitality and other expenses paid out of the missionary's family income. A similar situation was faced by the Eritrean Church in London, the Ethiopian Christian Fellowship in the UK during its founding in Preston, and even the Oromo Evangelical Church in London. These considerations will be dealt with in more detailed analysis in chapters Five and Six.

Planning

A cursory examination of questionnaire responses around the future planning of Ethiopian mission activity in Britain reveals a general lack of awareness of strategy or planning. A high number of respondents expressed ignorance about plans for the future of their churches. This can be explained by the words of one pastor, 'I do not make plans, it is as the spirit leads'. Another pastor remarked that in his experience, all the planning was just 'routine activity with no dramatic intention or significant change of direction or purpose', while another pastor wrote this cryptic response: 'By praying and by preaching the gospel and keeping fast pray.'[57] This may seem to show an apparent disregard for effective planning, but it is really an indication of the leadership styles in some of these churches. And yet here again there is a need to review whether this is a negligent leadership or one that is dependent on God entirely, even to the point of planning. It is perhaps too much to expect that churches will produce well-written business or vision plans in the same way secular organisations do.

In most cases, church pastors, by the nature of their office, play the role of a managing director or chief executive, often taking upon themselves the responsibility of the strategic direction of the church or mission point. Pastors therefore have much to do with any planning for the church, but how this will progress is as much about individual style as it is about leadership models. In a question about plans for his church's mission, one pastor simply said, 'I am reserved to answer this question to be honest all plan which I have submitted to God and we will see how the Lord answers'.[58]

There was little to be gleaned from this statement other than to infer that either the pastor had tendered his plans to God and was awaiting a sign to implement those plans, or that the pastor was being cautious; that after having put his plans to God, say, in prayer, he would rather he did not say anything about them until success was assured. It is perhaps more likely that the pastor considered his plans too sensitive to be divulged even for research.

---

[57] Pastor P T in questionnaire response.
[58] Pastor T H in questionnaire response.

In all the responses submitted on planning, all the pastors bar three had included an element of mission in their plans for the coming year. The key word used was 'evangelising' and 'new souls', while some pastors spoke about 'church growth' or 'equipping members for the preaching of the Gospel'. Here it is worth reproducing a typical response:

> The plan I have to make the church grow is through Evangelism to reach out the lost; through mission sending people to start new church; through worship; discipleship, and keeping warm fellowship among the body.[59]

The response above does highlight a slight problem, that in actual fact the respondent may have been thinking more about his vision for the church and not really providing a developmental or goal-orientated plan. It is possible that some respondents may have used the word 'plan' interchangeably with the concepts of vision, mission statement or even goals and objectives. In any case, such usage would not have diverted the intentions of this research, as what the research sought could be deduced easily from the answers given. In addition, a number of pastors clearly were planning not just for the present but were also making long-term plans, as in this response:

> There is five year strategic plan in place which the church is praying about and working towards.

---

[59] Pastor M G in questionnaire response.

> This covers spiritual work as well fund raising and longer term accommodation plan.[60]

The statement above, together with the other responses, clearly identifies one of the key purposes of the churches, which is mission. While most Ethiopian and Eritrean churches would like to see an increase or growth in membership, there is little evidence of a deliberate and coordinated missional programme in place. A number of pastors explained that they had some links with non-Ethiopian and Eritrean churches but these links were in most cases informal, or confined to churches with a similar background. In some cases the links were described as 'strong' while in others the partnerships had ceased. [61] For some churches, the sense of mission is marked by outreach. Hence the church is not a place for people to come to, but rather the opposite, a place for people to be sent from.

Evidence suggests Ethiopian and Eritrean churches have significant impact on cultural practices, but what is surprising is the subdued attitude towards mission and divergent views about cross-cultural engagement. The results raise a few questions for future research, not only about attitudes to identity, but also about the effectiveness of missional direction.

---

[60] Pastor T J in questionnaire response.

[61] From answers given by pastors in questionnaire responses in March 2012.

Chapter Five

Cultural Preservation or Cross-cultural Engagement

A preliminary discussion of the concept of culture and the way it is used in this book is necessary at this point. The term 'cultural preservation' has two or more possible interpretations, with negative or positive connotations. Firstly, there is the possible interpretation, in this research, of viewing churches as cultural vessels, transmitting a given culture, as it were, on a conveyor belt to a target group. Secondly, another interpretation is to see churches as custodians of culture. In this view, the church is seen as maintaining and protecting culture. It is however the case that churches may themselves be seen as products of culture, and hence serving a cultural purpose. As a missional movement, in my view, the Church is the product of a scriptural foundation from the time of the apostles.

Cultural preservation becomes a specific and often geographical or ethnic connection. If therefore the statement is made that Ethiopian and Eritrean churches are a cultural dead end, the implication is that the Ethiopian/Eritrean Church in the UK is beset by rigor mortis, an institution stuck in a lifeless culture in which there is no perception of what God is doing and which consequently fails to express the gospel of Jesus. At this point, there is no suggestion that this is the state of affairs in Ethiopian and Eritrean churches, and there is a need for more evidence and research to categorically consign Ethiopian and Eritrean Christianity in the UK to mere cultural vessels. Such a distinction is necessary in understanding mission, if the view taken is that mission is knowing what God is doing in the world and cooperating with him in doing it.[62] As such, knowing what God is doing in the world requires deeper insight or understanding of God's purposes, His will and His creativity.

The concept of culture

Newbigin is reported to have said that Western Christians need African, Asian and Hispanic Christians to help them make an analysis of Western culture.[63] By the same token, Ethiopian/Eritrean churches may be seen as permeating culture, bringing into traditional Ethiopian culture and identity the zest and life force of an all-embracing culture, i.e. the kingdom of God. In this view, churches are not mere vessels of culture but are to be seen as shaping and informing culture, and thus using this refined culture as an expression of mission. Whereas the relationship between churches and culture may have seemed to be negative, in this view, the attitude is to regard that relationship as positive, something to delight in, or at least, appreciate. Because of this, mission is to be understood as finding vigour within and outside the confines of culture. It is not

---

[62] Asamoah-Gyadu, 2008.
[63] Walls, 2002, p69.

bound or restrained by culture but it gives buoyancy to culture in order for one culture to reach out to other cultures. A definition credited to Bates and Plog from the field of anthropology, is that culture is 'the system of shared beliefs, values, customs, behaviours, and artefacts that the members of society use to cope with their world and with one another, and that are transmitted from generation to generation through learning'.[64] A dictionary definition refers to culture as a complex body 'of knowledge, folklore, language, rules, rituals, habits, lifestyles, attitudes, beliefs, and customs that link and give a common identity to a particular group of people at a specific point in time'.[65] In both definitions, culture is first a complex system, secondly it involves beliefs and practices, and thirdly it pertains to how a society perceives itself and engages with the rest of the world.

In other words, for this study, culture is about the beliefs, values, thinking, methods and practices prevailing in Ethiopian and Eritrean churches in the UK. Thus culture includes what the churches teach and believe about Christ, statements of faith or doctrine, patterns of worship, services, values and concepts of family, community, attitudes towards food, relationships, education, politics and so on. More broadly, in this book culture is meant as the sum total of attitudes, beliefs, practices and behaviours distinct to a particular group of people, including British society. Meaning is made in the light of culture. However, for the churches, the main and ultimate source of meaning

---

[64] http://www.umanitoba.ca/faculties/arts/anthropology/courses/122/module1/culture.html (accessed 19th January 2018).
[65] Encyclopedia of Communication and Information (2002).

is found in Christ, and in Christianity, which brings them into dialogue with other cultures outside or different from Ethiopian and Eritrean culture.

At this point, some classification of past and current nomenclatures is necessary. The term 'Ethiopian-type churches' is used in this book to refer to African-initiated churches. These are also known as African Independent churches or African Instituted churches. Ethiopian-type churches may have a connection with the Ethiopian movement of the nineteenth century in Southern Africa based on the rendition of Psalm 68:31 'Ethiopia shall soon stretch out her hands unto God' (KJV).[66] Apart from this, there is little connection with Ethiopia. In this book therefore, the term 'Ethiopian churches' refers to those churches with their origins in Ethiopia, whose leadership, adherents and language are in the main Ethiopian. This book does not make a distinction between African Independent churches and Ethiopian and Eritrean churches. This is to allow for specific church communities to self-describe themselves. The book is however concerned with Ethiopian and Eritrean evangelical churches in the UK with a shared historical, ethnic and cultural heritage and directly originating from Ethiopia and Eritrea.

Owing to the long history of black-led churches in general, African migrants are not creating a new religious tradition in Britain. There is now established a fair body of literature on African Christianity in Britain, distinct but not necessarily dissimilar to the evangelical family of Ethiopian and Eritrean Christianity in Britain. The core

---

[66] Haar, *Strangers and Sojourners*, 1998, p80.

aims of the Centre for Black and White Christian Partnership at Selly Oak in Birmingham was in practice the academic promotion of African Christianity in Britain.[67]

This leads to another term, Ethiopianism, which describes communities outside Ethiopia whose memberships are mainly of Ethiopian descent or origins.

Ethiopianism is concerned more about what it means to be an Ethiopian in the larger Christian community. This term might apply to the Ethiopian and Eritrean churches in the UK, although it is a term which has not been used in the research process. Over the years, Ethiopian culture has had to contend with new and external cultures. According to Barrett, Ethiopia played host to Protestant missionaries in the 1930s before it suffered military occupation by Italy.[68]

As was mentioned earlier, a large number of Oromo people in the UK congregate with other Ethiopians and hold their church services in Amharic. This apparent contradiction is connected to the influence of Islam in Ethiopia and Eritrea.

A closer look at statistics[69] shows a significant number of Muslims who are Oromo. In this instance, missional work is concerned not just with the host British community but also with Ethiopian and Eritrean people themselves. Mission can be said to be intercultural as well as cross-cultural. This missional activity can be illustrated as outreach within the one community setting, crossing from

---

[67] According to records at Company Data Rex, the CBWCP was dissolved on 27th May 2003.

[68] Barrett, 1968, p31.

[69] Adejumobi, 2007, p3.

one community to another with a shared history, and then crossing over to a totally new cultural community. It is a case of cultural dialogue, in which meaning is made while delighting and celebrating cultural diversity.

Ethiopian and Eritrean church leaders generally but not always share the experience of fleeing persecution and war. This experience is reinterpreted in mission terms as a response to what the churches see in their host country. As Ethiopians and Eritreans begin to find new meaning in Britain, they also begin to understand a deeper purpose for being in Britain, and this purpose is translated into mission. Mission is a response to a revealed purpose but made richer in dialogue, the aim of which is to set the human mind free to respond to liberating forces.[70] It is a dialogue because mission does not assume that those to whom the missionary is reaching out are a *tabula rasa*, a blank slate, but that there is something about the difference which can serve the whole. In other words, God delights in endowing individuals and groups differently out of His infinite treasury, in such a way that while each can claim to 'bear a resemblance to their common Father or Mother, none can pretend to have, on their own, all that God is able to give humanity'.[71]

So far in this research, the terms 'African-initiated churches', or 'African Independent churches' have been used. African Independent churches are said to constitute, perhaps, the largest black cultural organisations in Britain, mainly built and supported through genuine self-help

[70] Jehu-Appiah, 2003, p73.
[71] Kalilombe, 2003, pp68-69.

methods.[72] Sometimes in some academic writings, terms such as 'African Independent church' have been used interchangeably or even replaced by other terms, such as African-led churches and African Instituted churches. This is the subject of Barrett's detailed study in which he describes more than 1,000 religious movements in Africa.[73] Unfortunately, these terms do not serve the purposes of this research adequately. Ethiopian and Eritrean churches reject the commonly held notion that African Independent churches are syncretistic. It is neither a common or shared experience among Ethiopian and Eritrean churches to practice a watered-down form of Christianity. So a mixture of Christianity and other religions is unacceptable.

Syncretistic patterns of leadership are alien to Ethiopian and Eritrean Christianity even in the diaspora where they might be expected to flourish given the liberal environment. In contrast, Ethiopian pioneer church planters such as Getachew Zergaw[74] feel uncomfortable when addressed even by the title of 'pastor'. The term 'Gash' is sometimes used instead to address an older person or brother and denotes respect rather than privilege or power.

Terminology

The other difficulty is with the term 'African-led' or 'African Instituted churches'. Again, for Ethiopian and

---

[72] Owusu, 2000, p402.

[73] Barrett, 1968.

[74] Pioneer Ethiopian church planter in London and recognised leader for the past thirty years.

Eritrean Christianity, such terms only serve to highlight the legalistic nature of organisational governance. African-led or African Instituted churches are terms which are rejected because Ethiopian and Eritrean churches see themselves as led or instituted by Jesus Christ. By the same token, some Ethiopian and Eritrean churches reject concepts or descriptions such as 'Churches of Ethiopian and Eritrean origin', as they see Jesus as the origin of the Church, when He says 'on this rock I will build my church'.[75] For Ethiopian and Eritrean churches in Britain, the solution lies in dispensing with labels. Mission dispenses with cultural preservation. Instead, the challenge of the Ethiopian and Eritrean churches in Britain is to live in obedience to Christ and to live that obedience in humility. An approach resulting from this attitude does not necessarily reject culture, rather it accepts cultures as geographical and historical legacies which are dynamic and can only be refreshed and advanced by the light of the gospel. In this vein therefore, the missional approach is that of cross-cultural penetration. This point is suggested in comments by some respondents in which they say they have established links and networking with mainline British churches as a means to effective outreach. For these churches, they see cross-cultural engagement as involving the learning of English, the introduction of English services, the observance of English Church calendars and the acquisition of knowledge about being British.[76] This does not mean abandoning Ethiopian and Eritrean culture,

---

[75] Mathew 16:18, NIV UK 2011.
[76] Pastor N in interview on 12th March 2012, Leeds.

but is rather an indication that the UK is not just a mission field but a home.

Ethiopian and Eritrean churches engaged in mission reckon that in Britain, activities directed at fellow nationals within the United Kingdom simply equip such converts to return to Ethiopia as missionaries to their own people. In this scenario, mission roles are reciprocal. That is to say, Britain is both the mission field and mission base. Ethiopian churches, once the recipients of British missionary activity, have now found the original mission base their own launch pad for missionary activity. As Robinson puts it, not only is the mission base now a mission field for Christianity, it is a mission field in which Christianity competes with other faiths.[77] From Britain, Ethiopian Christians go back to Ethiopia and Eritrea and other parts of the world carrying with and in them the Christ. What Ethiopian and Eritrean churches see themselves doing is carrying on the great commission through mission. Britain, in giving a home to Ethiopian and Eritrean churches, not only experiences a new culture through Ethiopian Christianity, but also provides a fresh experience for Ethiopian and Eritrean Christians. This is a situation in which culture speaks to culture, and the medium which makes it possible for this communication to occur is the Holy Spirit. Britain, as mission field, becomes mission base once again as a new apostolate takes to radio, television and the internet, to broadcast and witness Christ to new lands. In being both mission field and force, Britain is the vital catalyst necessary for cross-cultural penetration of the message of Christ.

---

[77] Robinson, 2001, p74.

Walls discusses how the conception of mission essentially focused on Christ expanded to comprehend the work of the Creator and again to comprehend the special sphere of the Holy Spirit.[78] Mission is as much about the nature of culture as it is about allowing the distinct natures of God to inform culture. Both Ethiopian and Eritrean cultures have as part of their history engaged with Italian cultures. This is the heritage that both Ethiopian and Eritrean churches bring with them to the UK and through which they begin to engage with British culture. Ethiopian and Eritrean culture has directly or indirectly left a mark on the development and growth of Christianity in Africa, Europe, and wherever Ethiopian and Eritrean Christian pioneers have responded to mission. In doing so, the establishment of Ethiopian and Eritrean churches is not merely about cultural preservation but the use of culture in order to express Christ, to comprehend the work of God and the sphere of the Holy Spirit. In order to use culture therefore, the need for effective engagement between cultures can lead to greater appreciation for mission. This in turn ought to be an opportunity embraced by emergent Ethiopian and Eritrean churches in the UK.

---

[78] Walls, 2002, p256.

Chapter Six

Emergent Ethiopian and Eritrean Evangelical Churches: Mission and Vision

This chapter considers the engagement of Ethiopian and Eritrean churches in mission by exploring a critical element in the orientation of Ethiopian and Eritrean Christian leadership in the UK. Based on earlier research findings around the past and present development of Ethiopian and Eritrean churches, the chapter is concerned with the nature of vision or strategy in mission.

One of the challenges of the research was to identify the founders of the first Ethiopian and Eritrean churches in the United Kingdom. In some cases, a group of people would be indicated as the people who started the church. In other cases, there were individuals who played that leading or founding role. Based on interview discussions and records available, this book has given recognition to individuals from whom much can be learned regarding church planting. Each leader has had to deal with circumstances unique to their own experiences and situations, but much can be gained from pooling this vast human and spiritual resource.

Beginnings

The narrative research uncovers the history of the development of the early Ethiopian and Eritrean churches in the United Kingdom which can be traced to a few migrants in the early 1970s. Without the possibility of recourse to written documents such as minutes of church meetings and other primary sources, I have relied upon oral history as recalled by older members of the Ethiopian and Eritrean communities who are still alive in the UK today. It should be acknowledged that the first Christian Ethiopians and Eritreans to set foot in the United Kingdom did so at an earlier period, and that these Ethiopians may have been Christians from non-evangelical, Pentecostal or Protestant strands of Christendom. Suffice to say there seems to be a gap prior to the 1970s when a new wave of church planters arrived in Britain. Among the 'founding leaders' the names of Kassaye Degefu and his wife Maureen Degefu stand out. Kassaye Degefu came to the UK in 1974 as an evangelist and to commence a Bible college course, with the expectation that he would return to Ethiopia. Carey Baptist Church, Bristol, had sent Maureen as a missionary to Ethiopia. Mrs Margaret Ergate and Maureen Degefu served together in Ethiopia under the Red Sea Mission. Although Maureen and Degefu had met in Ethiopia, it was only in England that the two decided to marry. However, Degefu's plans to return to Ethiopia with his new bride were suddenly shattered when a new government took over. Degefu had no qualms about returning to Ethiopia having previously suffered incarceration under Haile Selassie's rule but with this new regime, he was not keen to expose Mrs Degefu to hardship and so decided to settle in the UK.

The Degefu home received a flow of visitors, especially ethnic Ethiopians. In 1983, the idea grew for prayers and some form of worship at the Degefu residence, which developed into an annual event. Among the early congregation members were Dr Berhanu, Drs Milkiyas and Tenagne, who had previously worshipped together as members of the Full Gospel Church Ethiopia. At the same time, there was an ongoing secessionist movement among various factions in Ethiopia, the result of which was the recognition of Eritrea as an independent country. Following this development, the previously united Ethiopian Church in London began to develop into two discernible communities. In 1990, the Eritrean Church began to meet as a house church, with Lia Mehari as the lead person. The precise details of the beginnings of the church are unclear owing to the fact that some sources say Mehari started a fellowship group with another unnamed woman in 1981. Other sources identify a small group led by Goitom Sium Mebrahtu as having led the formation of a new Eritrean church in London at the close of 1989. Mr Mebrahtu's experiences are discussed later in this chapter. Suffice to say Mehari was appreciated for her contribution during a Day of Reconciliation event on 3rd February 2011.[79]

For the Degefus, the decision to start an Ethiopian church was more to meet a need than premeditated. Their vision had always been to serve in Ethiopia. Even when

[79] The author attended the event held at the Ethiopian Christian Fellowship, King's Cross, London.

they were approached to undertake ministry work among Asian and Jamaican people, they declined as they felt their call and vision was for Ethiopians. However, there was no one they knew in Preston who was from Ethiopia! It was only through the local postman that contact was made with four other Ethiopians, and consequently from this initial contact with four people and a meal at the Degefu house, one man decided to 'give his heart to the Lord' on 23rd August 1977. This first convert was Zegeye Worku.

As a study in mission, the following factors sum up a continuum of milestones since the house group lunch fellowship meeting in 1977. From the baptism of the first convert and then the establishment of the Ethiopian Christian Fellowship of Great Britain, to the present day abundance of Ethiopian and Eritrean churches all over the United Kingdom, there has been growth. The church started with a couples' strong belief in a call and a vision to serve diaspora Ethiopians, and developed into the present vision to win Britain for Christ in mission. Growth has marked the life of Ethiopian Christianity in Britain. For example, the first Ethiopian church in Preston only amounted to ten members with an opening bank balance of £14.57 before spreading to London where it now boasts a church facility worth in excess of £2 million used by a membership of more than 500 Christians.

The decision to establish a fellowship for Ethiopians was made as a response to a social need. The fellowship started as a form of social action to reduce the loneliness experienced by these migrants who had left their homes. Today, social action is not only about providing a home away from home or recreating Ethiopian culture, it now includes professional advice around diverse issues such as immigration, debt counselling and health awareness.

Pioneer leaders

Understanding the development of Ethiopian and Eritrean churches and their missional endeavours needs to be balanced with a narrative about pioneering Eritrean Church leaders. The founding of the Eritrean Bethel Church in London is a case worth looking at. It is an evangelical church within the charismatic and Pentecostal movement. Connected with its early beginnings is a church elder and trustee known as Goitom Sium Mebrahtu. He recalled his first experience of attending church in the UK in November 1986. At that time, both Eritreans and Ethiopians met together once a month on a Saturday in the basement hall at Kensington Temple, part of the Elim Pentecostal Church. The congregation was approximately forty people of Ethiopian and Eritrean heritage with a mixed age group but very few children. The services were conducted mainly in Amharic but occasionally in Tigrigna. Having been part of this congregation and leadership until 1989, Goitom Sium Mebrahtu and a few of the Eritrean worshippers felt that there was a need to have a separate service targeting the Eritrean community in order to reach it more effectively. Another factor was that nationalist politics at the time meant that it was not sensible to continue with a service in both languages. As a result of this, the first Eritrean evangelical church, at that time named 'Eritrean Christian Fellowship in the UK', was started at the end of 1989.

Mebrahtu was key in laying a church constitution that is still in use. The challenges facing Mebrahtu and his colleagues may be shared by church planters today. For example, the availability of building facilities for the emergent communities was a huge issue because those Eritreans settling down in the UK had no community space to bring them together. The majority of the Eritrean community itself were asylum seekers with a variety of needs, from family and domestic issues to simply not knowing what the immediate future would bring as they waited for the UK Home Office to determine their immigration status. These pioneer church leaders did not have the benefit of an older generation of Christian leaders or peers to be relied upon and to seek out for advice. Mebrahtu and his colleagues adopted a trial and error approach to solving problems. In his own words, 'We needed to learn quickly and develop support network from our English Brothers'.[80] Their main constraint at that time, which continues even to this present day, was a lack of the resources needed to support the Eritrean community through provision of pastoral care and to spread the gospel as well. Because of this scarcity, Mebrahtu and his fellow ministers found themselves stretched physically, financially and mentally.

It is relevant here to mention Reverend Abera and Beletu Habte. They are an Ethiopian married couple who together established and launched the first and only Amharic Christian television channel available worldwide. Elshaddai TV was first conceived by the Habtes in July 2007 when they had the idea to serve God and reach out to

---

[80] Personal correspondence in letter dated 17th February 2012.

Ethiopians beyond London. Since then, its reach has grown considerably:

> There are lots of English language Christian Channels which can be watched in Ethiopia but not in Ethiopian national language. So the motivation is to reach our people with our own mother tongue.[81]

In order to resource the television channel, Elshaddai TV obtained the involvement of many churches, ministries and individuals most of whom sent material for broadcasting. Elshaddai TV does not only proclaim the gospel but is also a cultural medium. According to Beletu Habte, it contributes to cultural preservation in many ways:

> We produce programs when *bebeal gize* [festivals]. In Ethiopia from North to South and from East to West many people have a dish in their house follow the program. Nowadays even the farmers in remote area have a dish with a generator and watch the programs with local people. Churches in rular [sic] area have also a dish in their church and many people go there to watch it.

The success of Elshaddai TV is charted on its website in a way shows that Ethiopian Christians are cognisant of the advances and benefits of modern technology. It also seems to be a fitting adaptation of John Reith's statement

---

[81] Email correspondence dated March 2012.

about Christianity being the bedrock of the BBC. Furthermore, it shows that being a missional movement today requires a strong impulse and commitment as exemplified in these accounts of church pioneers.

Chapter Seven

Social Impact and Identity

In this chapter, I will focus on how Ethiopian and Eritrean churches engage with British society and their own communities in order to use social action to influence missional activity.

Haar (1998) writes that it is not Africa but the host community, present-day Europe, which defines the lives of members of African-initiated churches in the diaspora. In other words, the African response to establishing their own churches is predominantly a reaction to the host community churches failing to encourage a lasting welcome to these new arrivals. Often, mainline British Christianity has been quick to label these churches as syncretistic. This is possibly owing to a lack of understanding and knowledge of the Ethiopian and Eritrean Christian communities. In my experience, where ignorance prevails, suspicion and fear of new or emergent communities grows.

Refugee experience

Writing over two decades ago, Wallace observed in a study involving refugee communities that a number of those from Ethiopia and Eritrea, fleeing their homes in the wake of the fall of Haile Selassie, had differing levels of education, and that some Ethiopians and Eritreans were forced to become refugees while already in Britain. [82] Some who were students had to abandon their studies because the Ethiopian government terminated their scholarships, and others because of the war in Ethiopia. For these, it meant they had no qualifications, but here it must be stated that others did restart their education in some way. The point is that Ethiopian and Eritrean people resident in Britain have had an experience of social exclusion and disadvantage as traumatic as the effects of the war they have fled from.

It is not clear what the exact number of Ethiopians living in the United Kingdom is. Various figures have been mentioned and it is safe to assume that these statistics are intelligent guesses. According to the International Office of Migration (IOM) in 2006 there were approximately 58,000 Ethiopians living in the UK with London playing host to between 25,000 to 30,000 of them.[83] These figures rely on two sources of information, community leaders and the Home Office. In contrast, the Migration Information Source five years ago put the number of Ethiopians in the entire UK at 8,122.[84]

Part of the social action engaged in by Ethiopian and Eritrean churches is an effort to transmit the gospel in the light of mission, to go forth and multiply, to set the captives free and to declare the good news, according to the Bible. This is not peculiar to Ethiopian and Eritrean churches in

---

[82] Wallace, 1986, p27.

[83] IOM, 2006, p24.

[84] Terrazas, 2007.

the United Kingdom. Roberts observes that 'for the longest time, the primary response of the Church in the world economically has been charity'.[85] He perceives charity as a response embedded only in times of need; not as an ongoing concern. Instead, it is in development that long-term sustainability should be invested. Social action therefore should be offered or undertaken to meet those crisis points but the existence and promotion of mission should be seen as a long-term development. To state this in a different way, it can be said that acts of charity should constitute the exception while acts of proclamation should be the norm. It is therefore important to see social action as not merely papering over the cracks, but as part of the vocabulary of passion.

Charitable aims

The trust deeds of Emmanuel Christian Fellowship (UK Cities), a Leeds and Sheffield-based church attended by both Ethiopians and Eritreans, state that the church was established with two objectives: the advancement of the Christian faith and the relief of conditions of need or distress.[86] The first objective sets out the immediate and primary goal of this church, a registered charity. In this objective, the call to mission is explicit and the charitable social aims are covered in the second objective. The Emmanuel Christian Fellowship undertakes both aims seriously. There are weekly prayers for the church leaders, with each day of the week allocated to a named leader for

[85] Roberts Jr, 2007, p86.
[86] Lewis, 2005, p2.

prayer and fasting. The entire congregation participates on Wednesday evenings in intercessory prayer for the sick, needy or any stated requests. There is also fasting and prayer observed on the first Saturday of each month. Also, annually, during the last week of December, the congregation undertakes fasting and prayer. Other calls to prayer happen according to need. An annual conference is held, usually after the December fast, in January for three days. The conference attracts a nationwide attendance. This is in addition to the regular Sunday services held in Amharic and with an English service being developed to complement the Amharic service.[87]

Social action practised by the Emmanuel Christian Fellowship is generally similar to activities carried out by most community and voluntary organisations, with or without links to faith systems. The activities include organised football matches, social outings, trips and visits to the seaside or tourist attractions and are open to the general public. There are three major events held every year celebrating Christmas, New Year's Eve and Easter. Further celebratory activities are held to support church members' significant life moments, such as birthdays, weddings and funerals. As part of making the community more sustainable, employability schemes are encouraged and members may be assisted with job references if needed.

Another service provided by the church leadership is advocacy on behalf of the broader Ethiopian and Eritrean community at law courts for Eritrean Christian members

---

[87] Discussion with Leaders of Emmanuel Christian Fellowship, Leeds on 7th February 2012.

and letters of support to the Home Office if required. General information, advice and guidance are available to members of the community. Sometimes financial support for people in difficulty is given. Where the church is unable to help, a referral service is implemented. Emmanuel Christian Fellowship offers all of these services, but similar activities are undertaken in most Ethiopian and Eritrean churches across Britain as the needs of community and church members tend to be similar.[88] The undergirding principle in social action is that the churches see this as part of mission. Social action and preaching are seen as demonstrating God's interest in the day-to-day affairs of people. Preaching and social action are related to the pastoral care offered by the churches; both disseminate the salvic fullness of Jesus.[89] Ethiopian and Eritrean churches see mission as active, expressed in the narratives of

Jesus' chosen shepherds who teach or pastor as well as publicly tending to the physical needs of the community.

The objectives of Emmanuel Christian Fellowship are intended to stand alone but even when viewed together, they can be seen as embodying the call to mission. In the various spiritual and social activities listed above, cultural expressions do not take precedence over the gospel message. Ethiopian Christians are as comfortable dressed in traditional Ethiopian clothes as they are in Western clothes. However, when dressed in Ethiopian national or traditional clothes, Ethiopian or Eritrean Christians do so

---

[88] Discussion with Leaders, Emmanuel Christian Fellowship, Leeds, 7th February 2012.
[89] Ward, 2005, p224.

as a matter of preference and perhaps to add colour to a celebration event.

One reason the churches undertake these activities is to seek to make a difference, unwittingly contributing to what the Charity Commission sees as contributing to the public benefit, but essentially acting as 'my brother's keeper'.[90] Social action is interpreted or seen in the light of good works.[91] Because of what the Ethiopian and Eritrean churches see themselves doing, that is, fulfilling the gospel, the measure of the impact of the churches' social action in both the indigenous Ethiopian and Eritrean communities and local British or host communities, has to be addressed in a different way.

Being British

To understand the impact of Ethiopian and Eritrean churches on British society, one also needs to consider what is understood by being British. Being 'British' was described by 44 per cent of the population of the United Kingdom as their national identity in a social attitudes survey.[92] It seems the trend is for people in the United Kingdom to identify themselves more as English, Welsh or Scottish. Few organisations carry 'British' as part of their name. As Ethiopian and Eritrean Christians establish their churches and communities in Britain, the question of identity inevitably arises. Firstly, children whose parents may have strong or active links with Ethiopia, and perhaps

---

[90] Genesis 4:9 (NKJV).

[91] Matthew 25:33-36 (NKJV).

[92] Bradley, 2007, p7.

still consider themselves Ethiopians or Eritreans despite being resident in Britain, have a new or somewhat changed identity. Being Ethiopian-British may not be an option, but it is even more difficult to identify an 'Ethiopian Englishman'. Whereas most Ethiopian Christians are not particularly perturbed by questions of identity, some anxiety remains about the cultural heritage of their progeny, those children being born and brought up in Britain. If the host community is not at ease with its own identity, it may be argued that uncertainty grips those in emergent communities who are looking to start new lives in the United Kingdom and wanting to embrace Britishness. This is in part the intention behind the establishment of the Academy for the Study of Britishness at the University of Huddersfield.[93] It is easy to mistake African-Britishness from outward signs of living. Here for the sake of distinction we make note of the term 'Black British', which includes people sometimes identified as Afro-Caribbean and Asian. For example, one description is that:

> By day BMW cars, the ultimate symbol of inner city success, cruise up and down ... Occasionally you see the Rasta colours next to the Union Jack, signifying, perhaps, a dual allegiance, an emergent sense of being both black and British, with all the contradiction and tensions that go with such an identity.[94]

---

[93] This academy boasts various research and seminar papers on the subject.
[94] Owusu, 2000, p184.

Suffice to say that flying the national colours of one's country of origin suggests symbolic links with that heritage and yet the living-out of a culture, expressed in the day-to-day things of life, goes beyond the definition of nationhood. As a UK government census label, the term 'Black British – African' covers a multitude of identities and expectations and the addition of 'Church' only heightens the sense of heritage involved. The Church is important for most African people, sometimes seen as a 'bulwark against colonial, cultural and social domination'.[95] For a great number of Africans settling in the United Kingdom, Britishness offers the experience of the Christian mission base, the source of the missionary carrying the gospel to far-far countries once identified with Empire.[96] However, the prevalence of secular and plural religious systems may seem to be an affront to expectations. So how does the Ethiopian and Eritrean Church in Britain respond?

If it is accepted that the thesis advanced by Callum Brown is true, that the world has witnessed in these times *The Death of Christian Britain*,[97] it is necessary to find in the same text a rejuvenation of Christian missional movements. For Brown, formal Christianity is in terminal decline while secularisation is gaining the upper hand. This seems to be true, as more religious practices become the object of negative legal rulings.[98] Looking back at the 1960s, therefore, one could say that civil society has largely

[95] Owusu, 2000, p401.
[96] Bradley, 2007, pp186-87.
[97] Brown, 2009.
[98] Drury, 2012.

embraced secularism and marginalised religion in the public space. It is this cultural collapse of Christendom in Britain that requires a revisit of cross-cultural penetration by other cultures apart from secularism. What Ethiopian and Eritrean Christianity bring to British society is fervour and passion. Ethiopian and Eritrean church leaders need to find ways to engage that fervour in mission. The experience of a declining role of Christian influence is nothing new for Ethiopian Christianity. As Bediako notes, Haile Selassie's Christian autocracy in Ethiopia is gone.[99] And yet in practice, the Christian ethos has realigned itself in terms of outlook, culture, practice and space. Ethiopian and Eritrean Christian communities resident in Britain are now best placed to send missionaries to Ethiopia and Eritrea. However, it is only as they effectively address questions about how they perceive their identities that their mission can effectively trigger church growth within and beyond the United Kingdom.

Social fund

The missionary couple Mr and Mrs Kassaye Degefu have long espoused a social action agenda from the time of the inception of the Ethiopian Christian Fellowship in Great Britain. According to the minutes of the meeting held on 13th April 1980, the Ethiopian Christian Fellowship of Great Britain was formed in order to perform two overarching objectives: the gathering together of Ethiopian Christians for fellowship and mutual encouragement,

[99] Bediako, 1995, p249.

and to render practical help where possible. [100] The objective around practical help was further underlined by the resolution to open a bank account and set up a fund. This fund would obtain its income from members' voluntary contributions, calculated and set at 2 per cent of an individual's income. There were two stipulated uses for this fund: to cover costs for holding the biannual meetings or conferences, and to help Ethiopian Christians in need. Records show that four months later a subsequent meeting was held on the 10th August 1980, to clarify how practical help could be given. [101] At the heart of the reason for establishing a fund for social action, the Ethiopian Church in the United Kingdom was living out what it felt was crucial for mission, setting the captives free. [102]

Part of the social action conducted by the Ethiopian and Eritrean churches in Britain is aimed at restoring or promoting Christianity's obligation to disadvantaged people. In serving people who are disadvantaged, the churches provide a Christian message that traverses cultures: that mission always meets need. The need is for a gospel that occupies the void of alienation from the love of God and the need for an end to suffering due to scarcity. It is from this sense of mission that social action forms a key element of mission. Ethiopians and Eritreans seek not to impose an Ethiopian culture on British society but rather an emphasis on a renewed and shared Christian disposition. Hence social action is not about Ethiopian and Eritrean reaction to dire economic scenarios but a rising to

---

[100] Degefu, 1980, p1.

[101] Degefu, 1980a, p1.

[102] Luke 4:18 (NKJV).

the challenge of the gospel. In carrying out social action therefore, the influence of the Ethiopian and Eritrean churches has been really on emphasising a sense of identity in mission. The identity is that Christianity cuts across cultures and that mission is about establishing the kingdom of God wherever and whenever the church exists. In doing this, the Ethiopian and Eritrean churches first look inwards assuring young Ethiopians and Eritreans about their deeper and more fundamental identity as human beings, created in the image of God.

Identity

A call to Christianity is an appreciation of key values exemplified in another time by John Reith's statement, 'the call on which the BBC stood was the rock of Christianity and the moral code that flowed from it'.[103] Ethiopian identity is to be seen as based on the rock of Christianity, its Church, while social action is its moral obligation. In sharing such a conviction, it is not uncommon for churches such as the Emmanuel Christian Fellowship (UK Cities) to use radio and television in order to advance mission to a broader audience outside indigenous Ethiopian and Eritrean communities in Britain. Part of the efforts at cross-cultural penetration undertaken by members of Ethiopian and Eritrean churches have led to questions about Ethiopian identity in a way brought to the fore by the embedding of young Ethiopian families, and a generation of Ethiopians born in the United Kingdom whose relationship with Ethiopia is not as deep

[103] Bradley, 2007, p168.

as that of their parents. For this new generation, the churches have responded by introducing services in English while at the same time catering for the older members in Amharic or Tigrigna.

In terms of identity, the discussions held with several Ethiopians and Eritreans suggest that they see the United Kingdom as their home. They see themselves as permanently settled and have embraced the British systems entailed with citizenship. Unfortunately, the British Citizenship test is not seen as contributing to this sense of 'being at home' in the United Kingdom, and so there is a feeling that there is much more to how people identify themselves. In a discussion around the question of culture, there was a consensus about cultural activities reflecting identity but also a sense of acceptance, belonging and ownership. Part of this feeling related to values and even the 'blood in my veins'. The link between identity and cross-cultural engagement should therefore not just be seen in a list of observances of feasts and festivals, but the Ethiopian and Eritrean churches should also see these as important aspects of cross-cultural missional engagement. Through these, most Ethiopian and Eritrean churches do not see the need to celebrate traditional Ethiopian or Eritrean observances and tend to opt to celebrate British ones instead. It is worth noting here that the Ethiopian Orthodox Church still maintains observance of some of these traditional feast days.

The question of identity and culture is pertinent for UK-born Ethiopian and Eritrean children. Ethiopian and Eritrean churches in the UK could address this issue following a number of steps. Firstly, churches should understand what Religious Education is offered to children and young people in schools. They can use this information in order to bridge their children's learning to their faith. Secondly, churches should work with parents to understand and relate to the peer culture affecting their children. This could include understanding and using social networks as a tool for their learning. Thirdly, Ethiopian and Eritrean churches should be more proactive in establishing links with British churches and thereby broadening their experiences culturally and spiritually.

Such links can also help introduce children and young people to religious experiences outside their own communities. Another step churches should take is to allow for the active participation of young people in English services. Since most young people have a better command of English than their parents, young people are more likely to appreciate involvement in these services and develop more of an interest in them. There are several activities children and young people may want to do as a contribution to the missional work of their churches. This demands a leadership that is imaginative and able to find opportunities for their fuller engagement.

Chapter Eight

Recommendations and Conclusion

In this chapter, the research conclusion will review whether or not the research question has been answered. This chapter also serves to draw the various threads of the research question together. By drawing on the research findings and the data collected, this chapter will provide recommendations to help the Ethiopian and Eritrean churches address the question of cultural preservation and cross-cultural penetration in mission. A necessary aspect of this is to consider the gaps which have been identified, such as cross-cultural links, issues around the sustainability of the communities and missional training.

Earlier, we saw the research findings suggest that Ethiopian and Eritrean churches play an important role in the lives of their members and communities. The churches are seen as helping to promote or preserve Ethiopian and Eritrean culture although there is a growing realisation that a new and emergent generation of Ethiopian and Eritrean Christians also identify themselves with British culture. The origins of the first Ethiopian and Eritrean evangelical churches are in some cases uncertain. However, some church pioneers stand out as having played a pivotal role in the development of the churches. It can also be deduced that Ethiopian and Eritrean churches were not established in response to a missional call but more in response to prevailing social needs and the identifying of an opportunity to establish a church. This has often affected the way churches are structured and explains why there has been little effective missional outreach on the part of the churches. From the observations drawn in these findings, the following recommendations are suggested in order to avoid Ethiopian and Eritrean churches becoming a cultural dead end.

Owing to the paucity of literature on Ethiopian and Eritrean churches and my experiences during this research, this author feels compelled to argue for further in-depth research into Ethiopian and Eritrean church communities in Britain. This in part should help fill the chasm identified in respect of the body of literature on the issue. As mission becomes more and more everyone's concern, learning from the past and present can only serve to strengthen the Church and also hasten the establishment of the kingdom of God. Furthermore, the research findings are not conclusive in the sense that they indicate perceptions, intentions and plans that need revisiting and reviewing at a later date.

Faith

Very few Ethiopian and Eritrean Christians came to Christ as a result of the Ethiopian and Eritrean churches' efforts and none of those who became Christians are indigenous British. It is incumbent upon the churches to proclaim Christ in a more creative and imaginative way to the many people in the UK who are not Christians. The use of technology, such as mobile phones, the internet and television, offers opportunities which Ethiopian and Eritrean churches could use to reach beyond their immediate communities.

Interaction with host culture

Some interaction between Ethiopians and Eritreans and British people does take place but this friendship does not necessarily translate into gospel outreach. Church membership is made up broadly of Ethiopian and Eritrean people. Being a missional movement will require that church leaders and their members learn the English language as competently as they can, that they understand mission principles and practice, and that they develop the skills necessary to deal with today's issues. With this in mind, this book *recommends that a dynamic training mechanism is established to help prepare and equip churches, pastors and various ministries for cross-cultural missional engagement.*

Evangelism

There is a level of enquiry from British people about the faith of Ethiopian and Eritreans although this enquiry does not seem to result in tangible British converts. Connected to this is the finding that church members experience difficulty in communicating their faith due to a lack of fluency in English. Other barriers to effective mission are a lack of cooperation and unity among the churches, which in turn leads to splinter groups. Opportunities for engaging with non-Ethiopian and Eritrean communities are missed and the churches mainly focus on their own communities as mission field. *There is a need to identify opportunities for deeper dialogue among the churches and to establish networks or forums for church ministers to come together, offer each other support, counsel and share information.*

Social action

Social action is a significant contribution from the churches helping to meet the pastoral needs of members of the wider communities. However, as more and more Ethiopian and Eritrean Christians establish themselves and settle down in the UK and access benefits and other support through mainstream agencies, most of them begin to detach from the church. Social action needs to point to Christ rather than being perceived as an end in itself. This book *recommends that churches explore ways in which Ethiopian and Eritrean passion expressed through culture and identity could be translated into missional activity.*

Cultural preservation

The majority of respondents were of the view that churches play a significant role in preserving Ethiopian or Eritrean culture in the UK. Mission is said to be hampered by factors such as secularisation. Ethiopian and Eritrean churches make a relatively huge impact both on their own ethnic communities and on the host community. This impact may indirectly contribute to Ethiopian and Eritrean culture and be seen as external to mission. As recommended above, this book observes that the gospel uses culture and that the Church should always seek to understand God's will wherever it establishes a presence.

Cross-cultural mission

There is high dissatisfaction with outreach activities intended to reach out to the host community or non-Ethiopian and Eritrean people. The churches' cross-cultural engagement activity is not effective and there is concern about how the new generation of Ethiopian and Eritrean Christians leaders will be equipped for effective evangelism and mission. The issue of culture is complex and cross-cultural engagement is not just a replacement of Amharic, Oromiffaa or Tigrigna services with English services. In some cases, this may be a natural thing to do, especially in considering the needs of the young generation, almost all of whom speak English.

Cross-cultural engagement is also about the worship style, the manner of praise, attitudes to time, food, drink and of course language and thought. Consequently, this book *recommends that churches actively seek to establish cultural relationships and links with established mainstream British churches in order to achieve deeper and genuine cross-cultural engagement.*

Church leaders

A key strategy has been the use of English in worship and praise services. Some thinking through of cultural differences and negotiating culture-to-culture dialogue is still needed. Evidence suggests Ethiopian and Eritrean churches have significant impact on cultural practices but what is surprising is the subdued attitude towards mission and divergent views about cross-cultural engagement. Mission cannot be effective without a change in strategies.

Pastors should understand that modern Britain over the past twenty years has also changed culturally. *There is a need for church ministers to recognise their common experiences and embrace a shared strategy for missional outreach while respecting the lone voice speaking out from a different conviction.*

Unity

There are apparent divisions among the churches on various grounds, such as historical, political or ethnicity. Effective mission is often the result of God's invitation to work in cooperation with pioneering church planters, visionaries and other people. In order to truly bring this about, mission cannot seek out individual gratification but must seek the edification of the Church. This book *recommends that churches actively seek to work together to proclaim the gospel in unity and love.*

Resources

Several churches started without any independent or back-up finance. An experience of the pioneering church planters was the lack of resources in establishing those early Ethiopian and Eritrean churches in the UK. This is still a problem in mission today. One way forward is to follow the church-planting model as contrasted to the individual church-planting model. When established churches plant new churches, the burden of set-up costs are absorbed by the mother church instead of an individual.

This book *recommends that churches should take a more active role in establishing and sponsoring church-planting activities*. As has already been recommended above under the 'Interaction with host culture' and 'Cross-cultural mission' headings, it is my strong view that partnerships with host nation churches are very important and will offer significant benefits in terms of guidance, resources and training among other things.

Planning

Many church members have little awareness of outreach activities or strategies while several ministers have sparse plans for the future of their churches. The emergent group of Ethiopian and Eritrean ministers is faced by new challenges and demands different from those that first met the church pioneers in 1974. This is not to say all the early problems have been resolved but that there is a need to address the needs of children and young people with fresh resources and outlook, which requires some expertise. Planning is needed which embraces the new tools, skills, changing values and attitudes and looks ahead with fresh strategies. This book *recommends that churches must begin to invest in the leadership of the young generation by beginning to put into place comprehensive planning and appropriate training.*

Equipping for mission

The recommendations above represent challenges that are by no means easy and straightforward. Some of these challenges are a result of the way Ethiopian and Eritrean churches have been founded, the structures around which they have drawn their identity and the extent to which they have been influenced by changes around them. In order for churches to become truly missional, the first step is to advance the equipping of church ministers and members in mission. The most practical way of equipping Ethiopian and Eritrean churches is through training. There is a lot of training available with many benefits which churches should exploit in order to become effective missional movements. The importance of training is that there are various routes into effective missional skills. Churches could support ministers to acquire qualifications by attending classes at an institution of higher learning or similar. An option to achieve this is through informal study by reading books on the subject, research on the internet, watching DVDs and attending conferences or seminars on mission. A deliberate decision for missional training should help provide churches with the necessary skills for mission.

Furthermore, the equipping of Ethiopian and Eritrean churches could be undertaken in such a way that the churches establish a framework through which they share experiences around being missional and doing mission, and also encourage each other through peer mentoring. This could start with establishing a common register of mentors with a minimum set of standards and using these mentors to resource the churches and thereby champion the churches' missional strategies. Whether through training or mentoring, equipping churches may need to cover areas such as language, mission, communication, cross-cultural awareness and even leadership. For Ethiopian and Eritrean churches to be effective in reaching out to other nationalities, mentoring young adults and giving them platforms to exercise their gift is crucial.

Conclusion

The growth of the Ethiopian and Eritrean Christian churches in the United Kingdom has been steady and continues at a pace and focus that is still being developed. This research has been able to establish that growth has been marked by certain shifts in emphasis. In the beginning, the early Ethiopian and Eritrean churches saw themselves being called to respond to the spiritual, social, cultural and even economic needs of new or existing migrants from Ethiopia. The churches did not only perpetuate Ethiopian and Eritrean culture, rather they attempted to mitigate the effects of cultural shock experienced by Ethiopian migrants in the United Kingdom. In this way, Ethiopian and Eritrean churches have helped promote culture, but this has not been all they have achieved. These churches have also sought to be missional, learning and adapting to British culture as part of being Ethiopian Christians. This has been a challenge for most churches as they continue to negotiate what it means to be British. Being missional movements, Ethiopian and Eritrean churches are keen to reach out to others for Christ. This is expressed in intentions and planning but the importance of actively reaching outside their own communities is still to be understood.

The communities have a strong and identifiable sense of community which is translated into the Ethiopian and Eritrean churches. Given the need for proactive social action for the benefit of Ethiopian and Eritrean communities in the UK, Ethiopian and Eritrean churches feel duty-bound or obliged to undertake community activities to support their members. Such actions include information and guidance, employability training and language courses, to mention but a few. However, part of that mission is being translated into investing in young people as an ongoing response of the Church to God's will and purpose. By looking to the young for a more secure development of Ethiopian and Eritrean Christian churches, the churches are beginning to embrace host culture features, especially the use of English in services. In this way, the churches are pointing to cross-cultural penetration for mission.

The root of social action should be based on love; the proclamation of the Good News to places far and wide should be driven by a passion. The legacy of Ethiopian Christianity is a sense of history alive in today's missionary endeavours. It is about returning to a fearlessness, as experienced by Jesus' disciples after Pentecost. Ethiopian and Eritrean evangelical Christianity does not advocate a return to the simple things in life, neither does it promote a simple mind. Ethiopian and Eritrean churches seek to point to a deeper responsibility where selfishness, material gain and falsehoods have no place; it is about a return to mission.

Language is a key feature of Ethiopian and Eritrean culture; the same tool can be used for missional cross-cultural penetration, whether it is in Amharic, Tigrigna or English; the use of language should not end as a heart performance which proclaims Jesus; it should also transmit love and passion. Ward says that:

> language, too, must experience its Passion – that
> is, the central intuition of the economy of

representation, the movement towards naming
… Language 'expresses the gratuity of
sacrifice'.[104]

As missional movements, the Ethiopian and Eritrean
Christian churches in the United Kingdom see themselves
as Jesus' ambassadors and witnesses of His love. When
stripped of the divisive political and individualistic
elements which beset the churches occasionally, the key
contribution Ethiopian and Eritrean churches can make to
both their own communities and British society is the
embodiment of a loving and caring gospel whose
invitation transcends national boundaries. Most churches
have some plan in place regarding missional obligations.
But in reality, the plans of most Ethiopian and Eritrean
churches lack the depth and foundations needed for real
long-term growth and sustainability. Social action
embedded in cross-cultural engagement should
complement missional strategies embracing the new
generation of churches.

---

[104] Ward, 2005, p204.

Bibliography

Adejumobi, Saheed, 2007, *The History of Ethiopia*. London: Greenwood Press.

Aren, Gustav, 1999, *Envoys of the Gospel in Ethiopia In the Steps of the Evangelical Pioneers 1898-1936*. Stockholm: Verbum Publisher, Stockholm.

Aren, Gustav, 1978, *Evangelical Pioneers in Ethiopia: Origins of the Evangelical Church Mekane Yesus*. Studio Missionala Uppsala.

Asamoah-Gyadu, Kwabena, 2008, 'African-led Christianity in Europe: Migration and Diaspora Evangelism', online at http://www.lausanneworldpulse.com/themedarticles.php/973?pg=all (accessed 11th February 2012).

Barrett, David B, 1968, *Schism and Renewal in Africa: An Analysis of Six Thousand Contemporary Religious Movements*. Nairobi: Oxford University Press.

Baszanger, I, and Dodier, N, 2004, 'Ethnography Relating the Part to the Whole', in Silverman, D, 2004, ed.

Bediako, Kwame, 1995, *Christianity in Africa: The Renewal of a Non-Western Religion*. Edinburgh: Orbis Books and Edinburgh University Press.

Bell, Judith, 2005, *Doing Your Research Project – A guide for first-time researchers in education, health and social science.* Maidenhead: Open University Press, 4th edition.

Bryman, Alan, 2008, *Social Research Methods.* Oxford: Oxford University Press, 3rd edition.

Brown, Callum G, 2009, *The Death of Christian Britain – Understanding Secularisation 1800–2000.* Oxon: Routledge, 2nd edition.

Blaxter, Loraine, Hughes, Christina and Tight, Malcolm, 1996, *How to Research.* Maidenhead: Open University Press, 3rd edition.

Bonk, Jon, 1984, *Ethiopian Orthodox Church: An Annotated and Classified Bibliography.* ATLA and London: The Scarecrow Press.

Bradley, Ian, 2007, *Believing in Britain – The Spiritual Identity of Britishness.* Oxford: Lion Hudson.

Central Intelligence Agency, 'The World Factbook Ethiopia', online at https://www.cia.gov/library/publications/the-world-factbook/geos/et.html (accessed 19th March 2012).

Ethnos Research and Consultancy, 2005, 'Citizenship and Belonging: What is Britishness'. London, Commission for Racial Equality, online at http://ethnos.co.uk/what_is_britishness_CRE.pdf (accessed 6th April 2012).

Dawson, Catherine, 2009, *Introduction to Research Methods: A practical guide for anyone undertaking a research project.* Oxford: How To Books, 4th edition.

Degefu, K and Degefu, M, 2012, 'For it is God Who Is at Work in You, Both to Will and to Work for His Good Pleasure'. Preston.

Degefu, M, 1980, 'Minutes of Meeting Held on the 13th April 1980 at Silverwell Christian Guest House'. Morecambe.

Degefu, M, 1980a, 'Minutes of the Meeting Held on the 10th of August 1980'. Southport.

Degefu, M, 1984, 'Minutes of the Executive Committee of the Ethiopian Christian Fellowship of Gt Britain – Meeting held on 3rd November 1984'. Preston.

Drury, Ian, 2012, 'Christianity under attack: Anger as major court rulings go against British worshippers'. *Daily Mail*, 11th February 2012, online at: http://www.dailymail.co.uk/news/article-2099300/Councils-BANNED-sayingprayers-meetings-sparking-fury-Government-church-leaders.html#ixzz1n3K6qtqp (accessed 21st February 2012).

Encyclopedia of Communication and Information, 2002, 'Culture and Communication'. Michigan: The Gale Group Inc, online at http://www.highbeam.com/doc/1G2-3402900067.html (accessed 26th March 2012).

The Constitution of the Fellowship of Ethiopian Christians in the United Kingdom.

Fransen, Sonja and Kuschminder, Katie, 2009, *Migration in Ethiopia: History, Current Trends and Future Prospects.*

Paper Series: Migration and Development Country Profiles. Maastricht Graduate School of Governance.

Gerloff, Roswith, 2003, ed, Mission is Crossing Frontiers – Dissertations in Honour of Bongani A. Mazibuko. Pietermaritzburg: Cluster Publications.

Haar, Gerrie ter, 1998, *Halfway to Paradise: African Christians in Europe*. Cardiff Academic Press.

Haar, Gerrie ter, 1998, ed, *Strangers and Sojourners: Religious Communities in the Diaspora*. Peeters Publishers.

Holstein, J A and Gubrium, J F, 2004, 'The Active Interview', in Silverman, D, 2004, ed.

International Migration Office, 2006, Ethiopia – Mapping Exercise November 2008. London, IOM.

Jehu-Appiah, Jerisdan and Adegoke, John, 2003, 'Education in Mission: Reflections on B A Mazibuko's Teaching at the CBWCP', in Gerloff, R, 2003, ed, pp72-77.

Johnstone, Patrick and Mandryk, Jason, 2001, *Operation World When We Pray God Works*. Carlisle: Paternoster.

Jenkins, Philip, 2007, *The Next Christendom: The Coming of Global Christianity*. Oxford: Oxford University Press.

Kalilombe, Patrick, 'Black Theology', in *The Modern Theologians: An Introduction to Modern Theology Since 1918*, 193-216. Edited by David F Ford. Oxford: Blackwell, 1989.

Kalilombe, Patrick A, 2003, 'Partnership Through Education: Bongani Mazibuko as Remembered by a Colleague', in Gerloff, R., 2003, ed, pp61-71.

Lawson Lewis & Company, 2005, *Emmanuel Christian Fellowship (UK Cities)*. East Sussex, United Kingdom: Lawson Lewis & Company.

McLellan, Dick, 2010, *Messengers of Ethiopia Bearers of the Good News in the Omo River Valley*. Eastwood.

Menberu, Dirshaye, 2005, 'Onesimus Nesib c 1856 to 1931 Ethiopian Evangelical Church Mekane Yesus (EECMY) Ethiopia'. Addis Ababa. Online at https://dacb.org/sort/stories/ (accessed 26th February 2018).

Miller, J and Glassner, B, 2004, 'The "Inside" and the "Outside"', in Silverman, D, 2004, ed.

Pateman, Roy, 1990, *Eritrea: Even the Stones Are Burning*. Asmara, Red Sea Press.

Roberts Jr, Bob, 2007, *Glocalization: How Followers of Jesus Engage the New Flat World*. Michigan: Zondervan.

Robinson, Martin, 2001, *Winning Hearts Changing Minds*. Oxford: Lion Hudson.

Roxburgh, A J, and Romanuk, F, 2006, *The Missional Leader: Equipping Your Church to Reach a Changing World*. San Francisco: Jossey-Bass.

Schement, Jorge Reina, *Encyclopedia of Communication and Information*. London Macmillan Library, 2002 .

Stetzer, E, 2006, *Planting Missional Churches*. Nashville: B & H Publishing Group.

Silverman, D, 2004, *Qualitative Research Theory, Method and Practice*. London: SAGE Publications.

Temple, Bogusia and Moran, Rhetta, 2006, eds, *Doing Research With Refugees: Issues and guidelines*. Bristol: Policy Press.

Terrazas, Aaron Matteo, 2007, 'Beyond Regional Circularity: The Emergence of an Ethiopian Diaspora'. Washington DC: Migration Policy Institute, online at https://www.migrationpolicy.org/article/beyond-regional-circularity-emergence-ethiopian-diaspora/ (accessed 19th February 2018).

The Commission on the Future of Multi-Ethnic Britain/The Runnymede Trust, 2002, *The Future of Multi-Ethnic Britain: The Parekh Report*. London: Profile Books.

Ofcansky, Thomas P and Berry, LaVerle, 1991, eds, 'Mussolini's Invasion and the Italian Occupation of Ethiopia', in *Ethiopia: A Country Study*. Washington: GPO for the Library of Congress, online at http://countrystudies.us/ethiopia/19.htm (accessed 29th January 2018).

Owusu, Kwesi, 2000, ed, *Black British Culture & Society*. Oxon: Routledge.

Wallace, Tina, 1986, *Displaced Labour: A Study of Employment Among Educated Refugees From the Horn of Africa*. London: WUS (UK).

Walls, A R, 2002, *The Cross-Cultural Process in Christian History*. New York: Orbis Books.

Ward, Graham, 2005, *Christ and Culture*. Oxford: Blackwell Publishing.

Appendices

Appendix A

Questionnaire Sent to Ethiopian and Eritrean Churches and Responses

Part A: Copy of the Questionnaire to Church Members

Survey of Ethiopian and Eritrean Churches in the UK

Please mark your answer with a tick (√) inside the box of your choice.

1. Did you come to faith in:
Ethiopia/ Eritrea _____ UK _____ Other country _____ I am not yet a Christian _____

2. How many non-Ethiopian/Eritrean friends do you have in the UK?
0 _____ 1-2 _____ 3-5 _____ 6-10 _____ 11+ _____

3. Have your British friends wanted to learn more from you about your faith?
Yes _____ No _____

4. Are there any non-Ethiopian/Eritrean people you know who have come to faith because of your help?
Yes _____ No _____

5. What difficulties have you faced in sharing the Gospel with non-Ethiopian/Eritrean people in the UK?
Language _____ They are not welcoming _____ I am reserved/shy _____ Other _____

6. In your opinion, is the Ethiopian/Eritrean Church in the UK helping to promote Ethiopian/Eritrean culture?

Yes _____ No _____ Don't know

7. Do you think the Ethiopian/Eritrean Church in the UK is making a positive contribution to the community?

Yes _____ No _____ Don't know

8. Is the Ethiopian/Eritrean Church in the UK doing enough to bring in non-Ethiopian/Eritrean people to faith?

Yes _____ No _____ Don't know

Part B: Graphical Responses to Questionnaire in Showing Findings (in %)

Question 1: Sources of faith – where respondent came to faith

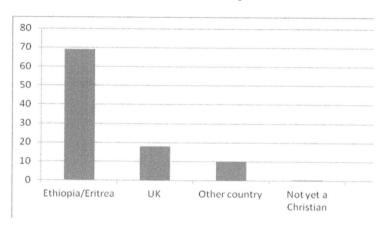

Question 2: Level of interaction and friendships with British people

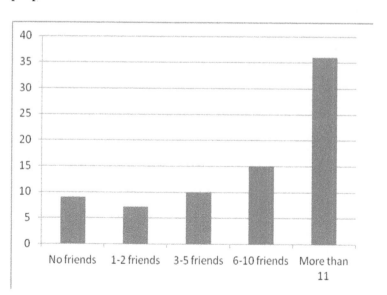

Question 3: Enquiries about faith from British friends

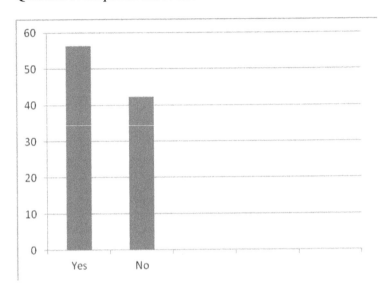

Question 4: Sharing own faith

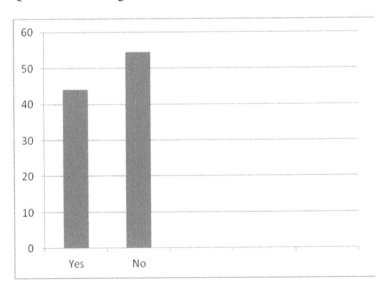

Question 5: Barriers to communication with members of host community

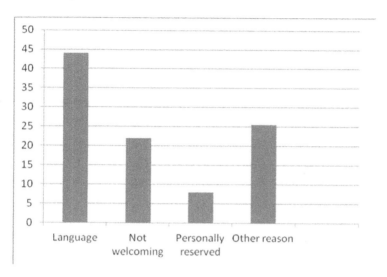

Question 6: Contributes to Ethiopian and Eritrean culture

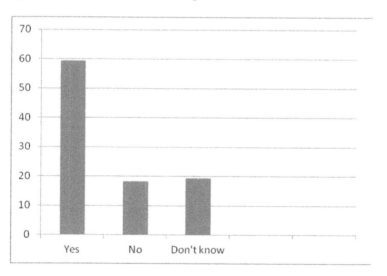

Question 7: Contributes to social action

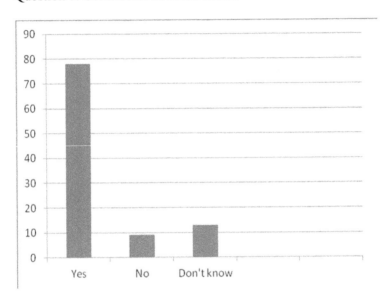

Question 8: Contributes to host community culture

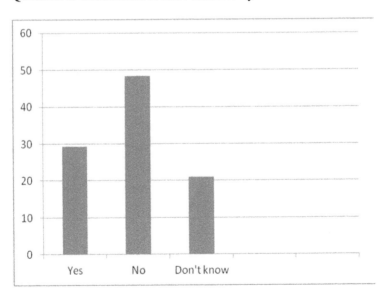

Appendix B

UK Ethiopian and Eritrean Church Pioneers Questionnaire

Part A: Copy of Questionnaire

UK Ethiopian and Eritrean Churches Questionnaire

Your name:
Your current position of responsibility in the church:
Name of your church:

1. Please give us a brief background around the following:
   a) What do you remember about Ethiopian/Eritrean churches when you first came to the UK? When was your first church in the UK started?
   b) As an individual, what was your contribution to the church in the UK? What inspired you to do this?
   c) What barriers did you face in ministry? How did you manage to overcome them?

2. Please tell us your thinking about the following:
   a) How has [sic] the Ethiopian/Eritrean churches in the UK changed from the situation you experienced in the beginning?
   b) Do you see an Ethiopian/Eritrean church in the UK helping to promote Ethiopian/Eritrean culture?
   c) How has the Church contributed to the Ethiopian/Eritrean communities in the UK? What about to the British community?

3.   From your experience/understanding, what do you suggest Ethiopian/Eritrean churches should do in order to grow?

Please send your responses by email to hirmmat@yahoo.co.uk by 20th February 2012 or sooner.

Part B: Responses from Church Pioneers

Please note that these responses have been reproduced as they were supplied.

Respondent: G S M

1.   Please give us a brief background around the following:

What do you remember about Ethiopian/Eritrean churches when you first came to the UK? When was your first church in the UK started?

The question needs to be slightly specific as the term Ethiopian/Eritrean church is broad. Within the Ethiopian and Eritrean churches you have the Orthodox, Catholic and evangelical churches.

My experience is mainly with Evangelical churches namely within the Pentecostal/charismatic movement therefore all view expressed relates to this church.

My first experience of attending church in the UK was in Nov 1986. I remember that the meeting at the time was held once a month at Kensington Temple (part of Elim Pentecostal church) on a Saturday in the basement hall, the congregation was approximately around 40 people of Ethiopian and Eritrean heritage with a mixed age group but very few children. The services were conducted mainly in Amharic but once a month in Tigrigna. Having been part of this congregation and leadership until 1989 a few of the Eritreans including myself felt that there was a need to have a separate service targeting the Eritrean community if we are to reach them out with the Gospel. The political situation at the time was not conducive to continue with the service with the two languages therefore the first Eritrean Evangelical church (at the time called Eritrean Christian fellowship in the UK) was started at the end of 1989.

As an individual, what was your contribution to the church in the UK? What inspired you to do this?

It is always difficult to talk about once self and contribution specially within the Christian sphere as we now that it is the Lord who leads and does things, we are his instruments. I would hope that through his grace I have been instrumental in setting up the First Eritrean church, laying a clear constitution and foundation that is sustainable and goes beyond the here and now.

What barriers did you face in ministry? How did you manage to overcome them?

Building facilities, as new communities who are settling in the UK there was a huge issues and needs of the Community that require to be addressed. The majority of the Eritrean community at the time were Asylum seekers waiting to hear from the Home office about their immigration status, there were no [o]lder Christian generation that can be relied and sought advice from therefore things were done more or less on a trial and error. We needed to learn quickly and develop support network from our English Brothers. The main constraint we had and continues to be the case is that the resource we had and the needs of the community that needed to be reached by the Gospel and comforted did not match therefore ministers and elders were stretched.

2. Please tell us your thinking about the following:

How has [sic] the Ethiopian/Eritrean churches in the UK changed from the situation you experienced in the beginning?

From the Mid-nineties with the huge number of young and new arrivals of Eritrean Christians in the UK, there has been a growth in the Church that was never anticipated if one was to look at the early 90's. We now have churches more or less across the Uk. There are also a huge number of British Eritreans (children born in the UK) been brought up within this churches (I am certain this is also the case within the Ethiopian church but my Ethiopian brothers can give a fuller picture). There are now Fellowship of Eritrean churches and are working towards developing a common ground in supporting each other and the community at large.

Do you see an Ethiopian/Eritrean Church in the UK helping to promote Ethiopian/Eritrean culture?

Yes but the church will first need to examine itself and agree on a common ground with regard to cultural issues, e.g secular music. There are a number of cultural issues that need to be retained within the community, I do not believe the church has yet reached this stage as it is trying to work on a common ground in particular with the challenges presented with the second generation, however once this is done it would be able to contribute.

How has the Church contributed to the Ethiopian/Eritrean communities in the UK? What about to the British community?

The churches main mission is to reach people with the Gospel and the church has done this as evidenced by the growth within the different Eritrean and Ethiopian churches. One would also hope that the community has been supported in settling to a new environment and society through the church. One of the other aims and purposes of Eritrean Beth-el church (the church I now belong to and is part its leadership) is to ensure that the Eritrean community retain its culture while also gating to now the British culture and make contribution. Our service includes inviting English speakers regularly and participating on outreach and other events with our British brothers and sisters.

From your experience/understanding, what do you suggest Ethiopian/Eritrean churches do in order to grow?

They need to take on Board the emerging and developing issues within their churches in particular children and young people issues. Those groups should be at the centre of the agenda for the church leadership and congregation and provisions made to reintegrate them to the main services at different levels.

There also need to be much closer working relationship with other churches within the UK and work with Evangelical sociality, Elim Pentecostal church and other Umbrella groups.

Respondent: A D G

1. Please give us a brief background around the following:

What do you remember about Ethiopian/Eritrean churches when you first came to the UK? When was your first church in the UK started?

There was only one church in London when I came to Uk and Ethiopian/Eritrean Christians were very small in numbers. I had planted my first church in London at the end of 1996.

As an individual, what was your contribution to the church in the UK? What inspired you to do this?

I have been contributed a lot in teaching and changing the generation. Since my teaching was based on faith and true knowledge of the word of God, many have been changed and have come to know who they really are in Christ. I did that because it was my calling.

What barriers did you face in ministry? How did you manage to overcome them?

My big barriers was from the church planted before I came to London. It was full of religious and cultural mind. Due to that, it had been very difficult to talk about faith. Because of that I have been passed through in many difficult situations. But praise the Lord. Since the one who called me is faithful, I passed all obstacles in His grace.

2. Please tell us your thinking about the following:

How has [sic] the Ethiopian/Eritrean churches in the UK changed from the situation you experienced in the beginning?

There is a lot of change now. Many churches has been planted and there are a lot of good pastors with good understanding of the word of God and the works of faith.

Do you see an Ethiopian/Eritrean Church in the UK helping to promote Ethiopian/Eritrean culture?

Yes. I can say that all are promoting Ethiopian/Eritrean culture.

How has the Church contributed to the Ethiopian/Eritrean communities in the UK? What about to the British community?

We all churches have a meetings and some of us has already taking some activities like sports and playing football among the churches. That will help more in getting together. Concerning the British community, the contribution is very little and lot of things has to be done to reach out them in every aspect of area.

From your experience/understanding, what do you suggest Ethiopian/Eritrean churches should do in order to grow?

Since they are working the kingdom, they should work together, respecting each other, accepting each other and supporting one to another. More of that they should show love for other sister churches and they should be role model for their congregation. We should break the barrier of the language and should get involve in the British culture and create a communications. When we do that, we will save the generation and reach out the ministries as well.

Respondent: E A

1. Please give us a brief background around the following:

What do you remember about Ethiopian/Eritrean churches when you first came to the UK? When was your first church in the UK started?

There is no concept of churches in the first thought but establishing a way we can help our people who came to UK.

As an individual, what was your contribution to the church in the UK? What inspired you to do this?

To witness to our fellow men and women so they can have everlasting life in Christ Jesus and to establish a fellowship in order to help suffering with cultural shock.

What barriers did you face in ministry? How did you manage to overcome them?

As an individual I did not face any barrier in my ministry but challenge which we face every day to serve our fellow men and women for the kingdom of God. The overcoming power is Jesus who said 'Cheer up I have overcome the world' [GW].

2. Please tell us your thinking about the following:

How has [sic] the Ethiopian/Eritrean churches in the UK changed from the situation you experienced in the beginning?

In the 1980s when we first came to UK our ministry our way of evangelisms was pure unwesternised way of thinking. As leader there was respect of one another respect word of God. As days gone by we became more westernised in our thinking like the western society. The western society culture has influenced into their way of thinking including our children and our ministry. That was great challenge we fighting not to give in even today.

Do you see an Ethiopian/Eritrean Church in the UK helping to promote Ethiopian/Eritrean culture?

We have great challenges ahead of us all as far as our culture is concerned. We have now another third generation coming up who are not even following either culture but new and revolutionised as modern generation that is our children. Are promoting the Ethiopian/Eritrean culture? The gospel of the Lord Jesus can change life but promote culture we have wait.

How has the Church contributed to the Ethiopian/Eritrean communities in the UK?

The church has played great roll among our communities in the last thirty years preaching the gospel of the Lord Jesus establishing fellowship after fellowship up and down the country. Today we are eye witness of all established churches and fellowship almost in every city in the UK. Did we contribute for community YES.

What about to the British community?

As Ethiopian/Eritrean community churches we have contributed for the British society in so many ways. We stood firm for our

Christian principle in worship, in witness and in our model of life. As I see it our Christian principle is firm on our believe.

From your experience/understanding, what do you suggest Ethiopian/Eritrean churches should do in order to grow?

The unity and respectability of the leadership is the key for the growth of a church. Brotherly love should be the heart beat of a church. The last command of our master before he died on the cross was love one another as I have loved you. If you love one for the other by this people will know that you are my disciples [see John 13:34-35]. This is key for church growth.

Respondent B H

As the first Ethiopian Christian Television Channel, what was your motivation in setting up the tv channel?

Our motivation was first to serve God and to reach our people. There are lots of English language Christian channels which can be watched in Ethiopia but not in Ethiopian national language. So the motivation is to reach our people with our own mother tongue.

How did you find resources to set up the channel?

We have many churches, ministries and individuals who are involved in this channel. They send the material to be broadcasted.

What was the initial response when you first started? What is the feedback at present?

No words to describe this. It is still like a dream for many of us. God has spoken long time ago about Christian Channel for our nation and when the time came everyone was rejoicing.

Do yourselves as helping to promote Ethiopian culture and/or spreading the gospel?

Yes in many ways. We produce programs when bebeal gize [festivals and celebrations]. In Ethiopia from North to South and from East to West many people have a dish in their house follow the program. Now a days even the farmers in remote area have a dish with a generator and watch the programs with local people. Churches in rular area have also a dish in their church and many people go there to watch it.

Appendix C

UK Ethiopian and Eritrean Church Leaders Questionnaire

Part A: Copy of Questionnaire

Your name:
Your title:
The name of your church:

Please respond to the following questions in brief.

1. a) When did this church start?_____
    b) Please tell us the name of the person who started it._____

2. How many Ethiopian/Eritrean (registered/regular) members are in your church? (Please write their numbers in the spaces below). _____

3. How many members in your church fall under the following categories:
    a) White British _____
    b) Asian _____
    c) Other Black British/African _____
    d) Other _____

4. Do you hold any non-Amharic/Tigrigna church services? If so please tell us the language(s) use.

5. Briefly explain what your difficulties are in sharing the Gospel with people who are White British?

6. List some activities you have done that have actually worked and helped you share the Gospel?

7. Describe the ethnic composition of the area in which your church is based.

8. Do you see Ethiopian/Eritrean churches in the UK helping to promote Ethiopian/Eritrean culture?

Do you have any partnerships/links with non-Ethiopian/Eritrean churches in the UK? Please briefly list these links.

9. Briefly tell us what plans you have, if any, to make your church grow?

Please use additional papers if you need to. Send your responses to: hirmmat@yahoo.co.uk by Monday 21st February 2012 or sooner.

Part B: Responses from Church Leaders

UK Ethiopian and Eritrean Churches Questionnaire

Your name:
Your title:
The name of your church:
Please respond to the following questions in brief.

Question 1
a) When did this church start? *March 1993*
b) Please tell us the name of the person who started it.

a) When did this church start? *2005*
b) Please tell us the name of the person who started it.

a) When did this church start? *1990*

b) Please tell us the name of the person who started it.

a) When did this church start? *Feb/2007*
b) Please tell us the name of the person who started it.

a) When did this church start? *2007*
b) Please tell us the name of the person who started it.

a) When did this church start?*15/05/2005*
b) Please tell us the name of the person who started it.

a) When did this church start? *early 2006*
b) Please tell us the name of the person who started it. *Started by 3-4 people*

a) When did this church start? *January 2003*
b) Please tell us the name of the person who started it.

a) When did this church start? *26 November 2002*
b) Please tell us the name of the person who started it.

a) When did this church start? *11 July 2004*
b) Please tell us the name of the person who started it.

a) When did this church start? *1982*
b) Please tell us the name of the person who started it. *A hand full of believers*

a) When did this church start? *Nov 2007*
b) Please tell us the name of the person who started it.

a) When did this church start? *November 2006*
b) Please tell us the name of the person who started it.

a) When did this church start? *Around 1994/95*

b) Please tell us the name of the person who started it. *Group of people, including ...*

2. How many Ethiopian/Eritrean (registered/regular) members are in your church?
(Please write their numbers in the spaces below).

Question 2
How many Ethiopian/Eritrean (registered/regular) members are in your church?

30 members
20
240
83 adults and 40 Children
30
15-20
about 150
55 Ethiopians and 120 Eritreans 175 Adults in total
200px
20 to 30
502
41 eritreans and 3 ethiopians
250 plus
About 50

Question 3
How many members in your church fall under the following categories:

a) White British *none, except visitors*
b) Asian *None*
c) Other Black British/African *25*
d) Other *American 1 Black Italian 4*
   NR
a) White British *0*

b) Asian *0*
c) Other Black British/African *238*
d) Other *Mixed race 3*

a) White British *0*
b) Asian *0*
c) Other Black British/African *0*
d) Other *0*

a) White British =
b) Asian =
c) Other Black British/African *30*
d) Other =

a) White British *0*
b) Asian *0*
c) Other Black British/African *0*
d) Other *0*

a) White British *None*
b) Asian *None*
c) Other Black British/African *None*
d) Other *None*

a) White British *Sometimes we have visitors*
b) Asian *None*
c) Other Black British/African *Sometimes we get visitors*
d) Other *Ethiopia/Eretria*

Question 4
Do you hold any non-Amharic/Tigrigna church services? If so please tell us the language(s) use.

Yes, English once in a month.

The church is multiethnic congregation around 40 nationalities and 300 + young and children. The majority of the church members are white British but it is also inclusive of West Indies, 40 Pakistanis 30, Iranians 46 and other African nationalities, and about 20 Eritreans.

Yes youth English programme and rarely Adults English programme.

No.

English bible study, ministering in English for English speaking communities throughout Birmingham.

No we don't hold any other service at this time but we are planning to start an English service in a near future.

No.

We don't use any rather than Amharic language. Some times when we get visitors we translate in to English.

No not yet.

No.

We do not yet hold any non-Amharic church services, but we plan to begin an English speaking service soon.

None.

Question 5
Briefly explain what your difficulties are in sharing the gospel with people who are White British?

Language barrier which we are trying tackle.

In our church we do evangelise for all people regardless of their ethnic and nationality. However the ethnic minorities seem to be more approachable and accessible as they have a need of immigration problem and the Church organise open door programs.

We have little commandment of the English Language.

Secularisation is working widely among them. In some instances they show a willingness to hear the good news and yet they are highly influenced by their day-to-day life concern.

Mostly language problems, and besides lack of cultural awareness together with high level of secularism.

We don't have any difficalities but they don't want to hear about the gospel.

Not knowing how to approach them and share the gospel in their own culture.

The language barrier, cultural difference.

Language, culture.

They are too materialistic and very ignorant to the Gospel.

Breaking past the cultural and language barriers.

Languages; cultural conflict; and some of them are not willing because of your colour; they are making themselves very busy; those are some of my difficulties.

As a newly founded church we are still in the early stages as far as outreach goes, and as such most members are focussed on personal development having recently found their freedom in

Christ. A few engage in personal evangelism, but on the whole (as well as church premise problems meant that we were not able to administer our programmes as efficiently as we would have liked to) we are still in the early stages.

Evangelism has a priority in our Business Plan for 2012.

I think language barrier is the main issue. Also lack of resources in terms of funding to do effective outreach work.

Question 6
List some activities you have done that have actually worked and helped you share the Gospel?

Gathering events invitation at Christmas, Easter and outings helped us sharing the Gospel apart from the church service and other programs (ie Sunday morning service and Bible study).

Open door program.
611 centre. (Stand for Isaiah 61:1 practical help for any one in need.)

Street outreach with evangelism group, conferences.

We had weekly youth worship service with different kinds of recreational activites. Mainly it was intended the youths who are living around the area.

We evangelise once a month throughout the major public gathering places of the city.

We have organised special events with anointed ministers from around.

Friendship and finding common interests.

We all love to pray for many ours.

We have create a team focuses on new comers both to our church and immigrants to Birmingham this team approaches them and help them when they are needy.

Preaching on the streets, helping specially new people the system of the country (one way of preaching the gospel).

Lunching club.
English class.
Maths class.

Evangelism activities.

Weekly church services and annual conferences where several hundred have come to faith in Jesus Christ over the past more than five years.

Main activities, apart from the regular church services include home base bible studies, youth group presentations and spiritual conference, women's groups quire and drama presentations, children's Sunday schools, prayer group activities.

Question 7

Describe the ethnic composition of the area in which your church is based.

The Church is located at the heart of London (city). Mainly offices are around it. In the area where resident are living, we believe the ethnic composition is British.

I believe it is a cosmopolitan city.

White and black ethnic groups.

White British.
Asian (Pakistani, Indian and Bangladesh.)
Caribbean

Ethiopian and Eritrean.

Fairly multicultural.

Martyrs Church of England.

All kinds of people from around the world including White, Black, Asian and so on.

In Birmingham, Pakistani was the largest minority group, followed by Indian, Black Caribbean and White Other.
The White Irish (52.1%) had the greatest proportion of people of pensionable age, followed by White British (18.7%) and Black Caribbean (17.8%).
According to ONS estimates the numbers of Pakistani, White Irish and Black Caribbean residents decreased between 2001 and 2009.
The Black African group increased by 14.3 thousand (223.4%) between 2001 and 2009, making it the most rapidly growing ethnic group in
Birmingham.

Eritreans and some Ethiopians.

More Pakistanis, India, people from 3rd world countries.

Multi-cultural (King's Cross).

Even if most of them are white Scottish there also many other ethics such as African, Asian, china, and some American.

Predominantly Caucasian.

Question 8

Do you see Ethiopian/Eritrean churches in the UK helping to promote Ethiopian/Eritrean culture?

Not to my knowledge.

In some churches I think I can say yes, in the bigger cities for the first generation it is OK to promote the culture. Hence, I'm not convinced and I have great concern for the second generation as they have a language and culture barrier.

Yes, there are some cultural influence.

Not really.

To some extent.

Yes.

No

Not really.

Yes, the right way to promot the culture is to make it accourding the word of God.

I don't think so. We are very close to our communities' member. It is very hard to integrate with other communities' member.

I'm not very sure; primarily the main focus is on promoting the gospel.

Yes but not effectively.

To some extent yes; all services are conducted in either Amharic or Tigrigna, therefore an important element of our culture – language – is being promoted.

No, this is not the aim of the church. There are other organisations whose main objective is to represent and promote Oromo Culture and Identity.

Question 9
Do you have any partnerships/links with non-Ethiopian/Eritrean churches in the UK? Please briefly list these links.

Yes, we used to, with Lutherans in Great Britain, but not any more for some personal reason.

We use to have a satellite church relationship with Kensington Temple.

We are working mainly with 'The Church of God of Prophecy' and with other English speaking church which are settled in and around Aston area.

We have a strong tie with Cardiff City Temple Church (Pentecostal Church).

Different churchs, Zinbabweans and Ghana and England.

Yes we have strong relationship and partnership with an English speaking church.

We don't have any links with non Ethio-Eritrean churches but we have a good fellowship with Assembles of God churches in our region.

Yes we have with Clapham Baptist Church sometimes we have fellowship together
(as we renting their building for our Saturday & Sunday services).

I am accredited a Baptist minister, sometimes I have got opportunities to preach in different English speaking Churches. I also have a privileged to attend local, national and International conferences and meetings.

Yes, we have connections with Kensington Temple Church.

Yes, with NIMC, New Mercy International Church

We have working relationships with CCPAS and a large London based church.

Yes, the OECL has very close links with Anglican and Baptist churches. OECL shares pastoral services and other annual activities with these churches. OECL also works with other Ethiopian churches and shares pastors and preachers regularly.

Question 10

Briefly tell us what plans you have, if any, to make your church grow?

Our 2012 plan is as follows:

> *Prayer and teaching that our congregation will become obedient in all that He commands.*
> *Encoring members to have the knowledge of the word of God, so that they will acquire personal spiritual growth (on going).*
> *Teaching the members that to reflect God's character in their daily life to the people around them, so that they will be attracted to our community.*
> *Teaching to the members to have a passion for the lost that is willing to go, to spread the good news to their world, because that is the first requirement for church growth.*
> *Outreaching as a group in the city proclaiming the good news.*
> *Building stronger the Sunday school by teaching the word.*

Using all possible technology to spread the good news (live internet TV preaching and teaching twice a week is our ongoing program).

Assisting the migrants and destitute people such as open door, 611 centres.
Multicultural congregation.

We are planning to reach English speakers strating with youth groups and thereafter to develop more English programmes.

We are planning to evangelise in different ways, for example, reaching the community in their own culture; promoting their needs; organising a recreational and sport activity.

Our focus is on giving more attention to new souls in providing a stronger follow up and the basics of Christian faith.

By praying and by preaching the gospel and keeping fast pray.

To extend our horizons to non-Erityrean/Ethiopian people, that's why we have a bible study that conducted 100% in English.

Our plans are creating a peaceful environment in our local congregation, equipping young leaders, building a healthy relationship with other churches ... etc.

We continue seeking the Lord on Prayer for Holy Spirit.
We give training specially in evangelisation.
And make people to preach the gospel even on the streets.

I am reserved to answer this question to be honest all plan which I have submitted to God and we will see how the Lord answers.

Continue with evangelising and equip our members with the word of God. Also, focus on the youth to set up their own English services.

The plan I have to make the church grow is through Evangelism to reach out the lost; through mission sending people to start new church; through worship; discipleship, and keeping warm fellowship among the body.

We plan to equip our members so that each one of us is engaged in personal evangelism.

There is five year strategic plan in place which the church is praying about and working towards. This covers spiritual work as well fund raising and longer term accommodation plan.

Appendix D

Minutes of Ethiopian Fellowship

Meeting of the Executive Committee of The Ethiopian Fellowship of Gt. Britain.

Meeting held on the 3rd. November 1984.
Place of Meeting – 50, St. Thomas Rd, Preston. Lancs.
Members present – Mr. Yohannis Yigzaw, (Chairman), Mr
Ergati Ayana (Vice Chairman.) Mr Kahsaye Berhe
(Accountant.) Mrs. Maureen Degefu (Secretary.) Miss Mesheret
Tefera. (Public Relations Officer.)

Minutes

1. The Chairman Mr. Yohannis Yigzaw gave thanks to Mr. &
   Mrs. K. Degefu, for all they have done in the past, for the
   Fellowship.

2. The Chairman then stressed the importance of the Members
   of the Executive Committee , experiencing the true love and
   untiy that there is in Christ among'st ourselves, which will
   then overflow to all members of the Fellowship. It was
   stressed that we are an Evangelical Interdenominational
   Fellowship, and that spiritual values are important to us.

3. It was decided that the Executive Council will meet once
   more before Easter, the date fixed is February 22-23rd 1985.

4. The next conference is to be held at the Christian Alliance,
   Southport, from April 12th-14th 1985. The cost being
   £18.40. The secretary is to write to all the members

informing them of this, and the application forms are to be sent out, early in January.

5. The Annual Conference is the be held at Oakhill College, London, from June 28th-30th. 1985. The cost being £20.00.

6. It was felt that the Conference should accomplish the following needs. All preaching & teaching should be in the Ethiopian language and cultural atmosphere. To encourage the development of real fellowship, and the giving and receiving of comfort where needed. Also to encourage each other to pray to-gether, the writing of letters, and to go on with the Lord in a deeper way.

7. Messages given at the conference to be taped recorded.

8. The programmes for the Easter and the Annual Conferences to be arranged by Mr. Ergati Ayana. (Vice Chairman.).

9. The detailed programming for the two Conferences arranged by the vice Chairman is to be discussed with the Chairman , then passed on to the secretary for any secretarial worx. The task of inviting and contacting speakers is the responsibility of the Vice Chairman.

10. Accommodation preceding or following the Annual Conference. It was felt that members of the Fellowship should be encouraged to open up their homes, and to help those coming from afar, especially those coming from abroad. This need is to be added to the application form and those able to give hospitality to let the secretary know.

11. At the Conference, the Christian v

12. Miss Meseret Tefera is to look into the possibility of cheap occommodation in hostels ect. in London area.

13. Those having any problems in attending the Conference to let us know.

14. The Committee has agreed to bear part of the cost where there is a real need.

15. It was discussed about setting a date and time periodically when the Executive Committee and Mr. Kassaye Degefu would pray and fast for the work of the Fellowship. For the time being it was decided to pray every Friday evening.

16. The responsibility of the newsletter would be Miss Meseret Tefera and Mrs. M. Degefu.

17. A sermonette is to be written by Mr. Yohannis Yigzaw, and distributed by Mr. K. Berhe.

18. It was passed that Mr. Kahsaye Berhe obtains headed note paper bearing just the name of the Fellowship and the office address. The Ethiopian Christian Fellowship of Gt. Britain 50, St. Thomas Rd. Preston, PR1. 6AX., Tel. 0772. 555738.

19. Usage of telephone at the home of Mr. & Mrs. K. Degefu. It was felt for the time being, that only the standing charge be paid for.

20. The problem of obtaining small Amharic Bibles was brought up. Mr Ergati Ayana is to investigate the matter.

21. It was decided that the secretary should investigate the matter of the Fellowship being listed as a charity.

22. The Chairman is to encourage the members of the Fellowship to reply to letters sent to them.

23. It was felt that reaching and encouraging new Christians is outside our work and it should be done by a Church.

24. Finance –

    a. It was agreed to continue to support Mr. Teklu Tesso by £20. per month until the next Annual meeting.

    b. If the Church in N. Ireland does not favourably respond to help Mr. Berhani Gidai the Fellowship to send him a love gift of £100.

c. Those in financial difficulties.With suport from the Chairman or Vice Chairman, up to a maxium of £100 is able to be given.

25. <u>Public Relations</u> –

   a. It was thought good to write to Qais Ezera and to invite him and his family to come and share fellowship, and to pass on news of other Ethiopian Fellowships in Europe.

   b. Independently to write to Yewerkwoha Beyana, and to ask her to pass on news from other Fellowships.

   c. To write to Tewelde Yohannis & family and Fereweyne Fernengel, both in W. Germany, inviting them to come and pass their news onto us.

   d. To contact Tega (France) and share fellowship with us.

   e. Ethiopians Christians in N. Ireland to be contacted by Kassaye Berhe and Yohannis Yigzaw

   f. A letter introducing the Fellowship to be written to Bible Colleges and Universities.

   g. Contacting Ethiopian, in the Communistic Bloc. It was decided that Yohannis is to write a letter, Mr. K. Degefu to write it in Amharic, and Mrs. M. Degefu, to send them out.

The meeting finished for 6pm, we then all enjoyed an Ethiopian meal of Injera & Wot.

Appendix E

First Constitution of Ethiopian Fellowship

The Constitution of the Fellowship Christians in the United Kingdom.

Article I.

Name

The Fellowship shall be called the 'Fellowship of Ethiopian Christians in the United Kingdom.'

Article II.

Purpose.

1. To create a Fellowship among Ethiopian Christians in the United Kingdom and the Continent.

2. To encourage Ethiopian Christians in the United Kingdom in their daily Christian living.

3. To help Ethiopian Christians with their different problems through prayer & other means possible,

4. To bear a witness to the Lord Jesus Christ to Ethiopian non Christians.

Article III.

Doctrinal Stand

1. The Fellowship maintains that the Bible is the inspired Word of God and that salvation is only through faith in Jesus Christ.

2.   The Fellowship is inter-denominational and hence shall not make distinction between denominations that have Bible based doctrines.

Article IV.

Membership

Ethiopians that are born again Christians, who accept article III may be members of the Fellowship.

All non-Ethiopian Christians spouses may also be members.

Ex-missionaries to Ethiopia may be accepted as associate members.

Article V.

Organization

1.   The General Conference is the supreme body of the Fellowship.

2.   The activities of the association shall be governed by the Executive body elected at the General Conference.

3.   The Executive body shall comprise of –

   a.   Chairman.
   b.   Vice Chairman.
   c.   Treasurer.
   d.   Secretary.
   e.   Public relations Officer.

4.   All decisions shall be made by simple majority vote.

5.   All Officers are elected for two years and may be re-elected. Elections shall be conducted in such a way that some of the previous Officers will still be in Office when new Officers are appointed.

Article VI.

Finance.

1. Every member is expected to contribute a covenanted amount per month to the Fellowship. However, the Fellowship shall depend upon God for its finance.

2. The Treasurer shall send an official receipt acknowledging every gift recieved.

3. The account of the Fellowship shall be kept in a bank in the name of the two of the members of the executive committee and withdrawals shall be made in the name of two persons or as required by the bank.

Article VIII.

Expenses.

A. Travelling and other expenses incurred by the executive committee members, for a committee meeting or the like, shall be refunded by the Fellowship if the need arises.

B. The executive committee shall allocate a lump sum of money that can be used on telephone, postal and other correspondence expenses and for emergency use.

C. All expenses covered by the Fellowship must be fully approved by the executive committee.

D. On the approval of at least two thirds of the members of the executive committee, the Fellowship may give financial support for any its members who are in desperate need. Though the amount of money to be given at any one time depends on the availability and the circumstances, it may not exceed £100.00.

Article XI.

General Conference.

A. The Fellowship shall have one Annual General Conference at a central place.

B. The Fellowship may have a second General Conference.

C. All business meetings, revisions of the constitution, election of Officers can only be carried out at the recognised Annual General Conference.

Article X.

Revision of the Constitution.

This constitution may be revised as required to suit the functions of the Fellowship better.

Appendix F

Narrative from the Degefus

"For it is God who is at work in you, both to will and to work for his good pleasure." Phil. 2.ver.13

What ever we do for God it is not of us that we do the work, but it is God who does the work himself. In another place the apostle Paul tells us, that whether it is planting of a Church or a different ministry in the Church with different gifts, it is God who does all the work. 1Cor.3.ver.5-8, 12.ver.4-7,11. In other word we are nothing but God is everything in all things.

As we all know very well, in the past God used people or Animals to do his will and fulfil his purposes. E.g. the ravens to feed Elijah the prophet or the lepers to bring good news to the besieged people in Samaria, in order to relieve the people from famine. Also Joseph was another who was used by God. Both Joseph and the lepers did not have a clear call or a vision from God, but their circumstances lead them into service to be used by God. Looking back our ministry is similar to that of Joseph, who was sent by his father to enquire about his brothers and to return back to his home. Joseph's story tells us how he was prevented from returning home, and ended up in a foreign country. When I arrived in the U.K in 1974 I expected to return to Ethiopia as soon I finished Bible College. As we all know the situation in Ethiopia changed quickly in the same year and we were prevented from returning home. Personally I was not worried about returning home, as under the Emperor Haile Selassie's rule I had been in prison many times for being an Evangelist, but could not return and take Maureen with me into hardship. As I could not return home I was down and very discouraged. All I could do was to pray and ask the Lord for his leading and direction. As I have mentioned earlier I was an Evangelist and Maureen was a Missionary in Ethiopia. In those days the only vision that we had was to serve Ethiopians. The problem that we had here in Preston, we thought we were the only Ethiopians who lived in the area.

Our Church here in Preston who had supported us, realising our potential for ministry asked us to work among the Asians and Jamaicans, supporting us fully. But we told them, that we didn't have a call or a vision for these people. The call and vision, that we have was for Ethiopians. The problem was we didn't know anyone in Preston or in this part of the country. The church accepted our decision and kept praying for us.

Suddenly out of the blue our postman started talking to us about our background due to our surname. When we mentioned the fact that I was from Ethiopia, he told us that there were four Ethiopians living in Preston but he wasn't allowed legally to give us their addresses, but told us roughly the area they lived. Eventually we went to the area and found one of them, called Getaneh in a small flat. While we were talking to him another one appeared. His name is Zegeye. They told us, that they were attending the Radio School for Maritime communications in Preston. Finally we invited them to hour house for a meal. Later the other two joined us. We witnessed to all of them concerning the love of God and saving the power of Jesus Christ. One of them even attended few conferences but never gave his heart to the Lord. I think he was after girls not after Christ.

Out of the four we became close to one family. His name is Zegeyie Worku. Eventually 23rd of August 1977 he gave his heart to the Lord. That was a great encouragement to us and a confirmation to us; at that time our call was to the Ethiopians. Later on we came into contact with Dr. Abraham Araya as we were entering a building for a conference, which was arranged by young people In Liverpool. He was a student at Salford University. As I had never met Abraham before in Ethiopia, I said to Maureen he looks like an Ethiopian. And she said to me, go and ask him. At the end of the meeting we exchanged our addresses and invited him to come to see us. He used to come to see us whenever he had a free time, and we had a sweet fellowship between us. It was a great encouragement to all of us. Another times Abraham would bring other Ethiopians who were visiting him. In those days he was very generous in supporting the fellowship.

To our surprise four Ethiopians who had known me in Ethiopia suddenly arrived in different part of the U.K Dr. Berhanu, Dr. Milkias and Tenagne Lemma arrived in Glasgow and Tekeste Tekle arrived in Birmingham. This is around 1979? To this day I don't know how they found my address. Out of the four, the first one who came to visit us was Tekeste. We think it was he who gave our address to the rest in Glasgow. By now Abraham had moved to Edinburgh University. Tekeste stayed with us for a week. As I knew him in Ethiopia, that he was very good in helping and teaching young Christians I wanted him to stay with Zegeye most of the days that he spent with us.

In November 1979 for the first time they all came to our home for a weekend from different places. Also Egigayu came from London. All in all we were 9. Mellesse visited us earlier in the 1975, 1976? as a friend, but didn't come this time. However he attended the next conference in Morecambe at Easter 1980. It was suggested at this weekend gathering, Maureen to find a place for a weekend to have a fellowship in Amharic. So the first conference was held at the Silverwell Christian Guest House in Morecambe, this was at Easter April 1980. At the Morecambe conference people came from Bath and Swansea. Also a missionary who had worked in Ethiopia who we didn't know attended the meeting. At the conference Fikedu, a student from Bath University gave a testimony how he was so depressed and felt lonely because of cultural shock & lack of Ethiopian fellowship. He told us, that how encouraged he was by coming to the meeting. We were in tears when we heard his testimony. At this meeting we made decision for the future fellowship. The minutes were as follows:-

MINUTES OF MEETING HELD ON THE 13th APRIL 1980

PLACE OF MEETING The Silverwell Christian Guest House, Morecambe

MEMBERS PRESNT   10

MATTERS ARISING

(1) OUR NAME   the decision was made by the members to call ourselve The Ethiopian Christian Fellowship of Great Britain
(2) AIMS OF THE FELLOWSHIP
    (a) For Ethiopian Christians to gather together for fellowship and to encourage one other.
    (b) To write and keep in contact as much as possible with each other and those Ethiopian brothers and sisters who are isolated around the country and can't meet.
    (c) To help in practical matters as far as possible.
(3) GIVING
It was decided that 2% of a persons income (voluntary) to be given to the fellowship, to cover conference expenses and to help Ethiopian Christians in need.

THE FOLLOWING WERE ELECTED BY THE MEMBERS PRESENT AT THE MEETING
(1) TREASURER   MR KASSAYE DEGEFU
                      MR ZEGEYE WORKU
The Bank was opened straight away after the conference in April 1980 with deposit of £14.57.

(2) HOST & HOSTESS   Mr. & Mrs. K. DEGEFU

(3) SECRETARY   Mrs M DEGEFU

At this meeting we also decided to have conferences twice a year. One at Easter and the other one in August. As the Silverwell Christian Guest House in Morecambe was not big enough for the weekend we then moved to the Christian Alliance Hotel in Southport in August 1980. This time the members present was 11. Also another missionary who had work in Ethiopia, Miss. Hazel Collin from Bristol attended the conference. She was willing to help to contact any Ethiopian in the south of England.

MINUTS OF THE MEETING HELD ON THE 10th OF AUGUST 1980

PLACE OF MEETING THE CHRISTIAN ALLIANCE HOTEL SOUTHPORT, LANCS.

MEMBERS PRESENT 11

(1) AMENDMENT TO NO 4. OF PREVIOUS MEETING.

Due to formalities at the Westminster Bank, Mr. Kassaye Degefu is listed as Treasurer and Mr. Zegeye Worku to sign on the Cheque as a member of the Ethiopian Christian Fellowship of Great Britain. The Bank was already opened in April 1980 as it is mentioned above.

(2) MATTERS AROSE HOW TO HELP IN PRACTICAL MATTERS?

    (a) When a need is known share it.
    (b) Visit if possible.
    (c) If financial help is requested the visitor is to let the Treasurer know and the help to be given while visiting if possible.

A year Ergate from Scotland and Messeret and Migbar from London joined us. Messeret was very helpful in many ways specially in playing the Guitar. Without her playing the Guitar the singing would have been dull and monotonous. Later in 1982 at conference, held at London Bible College, she was elected to be representative for the south of Britain. Also she was elected to serve the Fellowship as member of the committee. As the same time Ergate was elected to be representative the Northern area. In those early days Ergate and Messeret were very vital for the fellowship to take off the ground. Ergate began to bring many students from Glasgow University. As a result at one of the conference at Southport one student gave his heart to the Lord at the end of the conference. Soon the group in Glasgow started having fellowship with one another.

Later Yohanis Gizew from Northern Ireland and Getachew Zeregaw from Reading joined us. They were well experienced in serving the Lord back in Ethiopia. Being a man of wisdom and experience in God's work Yohanis made a great contribution to the fellowship especially when the constitution was written. Getachew was elected at the London conference in 1983 as member of the committee then he was elected by the committee as chairman and head up the fellowship in London. The numbers grew rapidly, as many began coming from London. For some years 2 conferences were held, one at Easter in Southport and one in July or in August in London. Soon some Ethiopians began to attend conferences from Europe and from Scandinavian counties, such as from Sweden. Some went back and as a result they were encouraged to start their own fellowship. E.g. Tadesse Dejene in Holland, Guim, after finishing his course at Loughborough University returned to Norway and started the fellowship in Oslo. I was privileged to speak, both in Holland and in Norway at their conferences. As a result the contact and fellowship with the European Ethiopian Brothers and Sisters had began.

We continued to serve the fellowship until 1994, in the latter part from 1992–1994 as Trustees. As my ministry is pioneering a work we felt the time had come to pass over the work to the

London group, as the work there was well established by this time.

We began to pray for the Lord to guide us to a new ministry, and he has opened for us a new door to serve him.

Over the years it has been an encouragement to hear how the work in London has gone from strength to strength. As it started with small beginnings how little how little did we realise it would become a great work for the Lord. Looking back when the fellowship was started, there was no tribal or denominational, barriers people were just hungry for fellowship with one another. To-day people are hungry to start their own fellowship. They split the fellowship and start another. This is a worldwide problem, not just a nationwide problem. Although one may not know the real motive of an individual according to scripture these are the two main reasons. First, it is a lack of maturity and spirituality. **1. Cor. 3. ver. 1-5, 13. ver. 11-13**. Secondly, it is selfish ambition **Phl. 1.ver. 15-17**. As Apostle Paul was telling us, that if we look in a mirror, we only see ourselves, but if we look to the Lord we will see our selves as the prophet Isaiah saw him self Is. 6.vr.1-5.

The fellowship is only 25 years old, still young and not yet fully matured. We pray that it may continue to increase in numbers, spiritual growth and in maturity.

Kassaye & Maureen

Appendix G

A Chronological History of the Development of Ethiopian and Eritrean Churches in UK

1974 – Pioneer Kassaye came to the UK.

1977 – Kassaye met other Ethiopians in Preston through local postman; first convert (23rd November), Zegeye Worku.

1979 – November, the first meeting (nine people) at Kassaye's, Preston c 1979. Arrival of others: Dr Berhanu, Dr Milkias and Tenagne arrived in Glasgow – Tekste in Birmingham.

1980 – Second meeting in Morecambe (ten people).

April 1980 – First official Ethiopian Fellowship held at the Silverwell Christian Guest House, Morecambe (minutes).

Aug 1980 – Another meeting at the Christian Alliance Hotel, Southport, Lancashire (eleven people).

1981 – Joining of other Christian ministers in Preston: Ergate Ayana from Scotland and Meseret and Migbar from London.

1982 – Conference held at London Bible College. Meseret elected representative of south Britain. Ergate Ayana elected to be representative of the northern area.

Late 1982 – Yohanis Gizew from Ireland and Getachew Zergaw from Reading join the fellowship.

1983 – London conference, Getachew Zergaw elected chairman of committee and head of the Fellowship in London.

Late 1989 – Eritrean Christian Fellowship established at Lia Mehari's house.

1990 – Bethel Eritrean Church established in London.

March 1993 – Ethiopian Evangelical Church – Mekane Yesus in London – established by Reverend Barnabas Daniel.

1994/95 – Oromo Evangelical Church of London established.

1995 – Emmanuel Ethiopian Evangelical Christian Fellowship established.

Late 1996 – Righteousness Faith Ministry, London established by Daniel Getachew.

2000 – Rhema Faith Ministries established in London, established by Zewude Gebresilassie.

Nov 2002 – Hebron Apostolic and Prophetic Church, London established.

Jan 2003 – Emmanuel Christian Fellowship UK Cities, Leeds established by Hirpo Kumbi.

Jan 2003 – Rhema Faith Ministries established in Birmingham by Zewude Gebresilassie and his apostolic team.

Dec 2003 – Rehma Faith Ministries established in Manchester by Zewude Gebresilassie and apostolic team.

Oct 2004 – Emmanuel Christian Fellowship UK Cities, Sheffield established by Hirpo Kumbi.

Jul 2004 – Grace Gospel Church established in Leeds by Terefe Tedesse.

Jan 2004 – Rehma Faith Ministries established in Leeds by Zewude Gebresilassie and his apostolic team.

2004 – Rehma Faith Ministries established in Portsmouth by Zewude Gebresilassie and his apostolic team.

2004 – Rehma Faith Ministries established in Coventry by Zewude Gebresilassie and his apostolic team.

2004 – Gospel Truth Ministries International established by Fekedu and Tiru Tegegn.

May 2005 – The Church of Christ International Faith Ministries established at Leicester by Misgina Segid.

2005 – Church of the Living God established at Sheffield by Habtom Mirach.

2005 – Rehoboth Elim Church established in Birmingham by Girma Sahilu.

Early 2006 – Assembly of the Brethren in Christ Church established in Birmingham by Bethel Eritrean Church of London.

Nov 2006 – Holiness Unto the Lord International Church established in London by Zinaw Tesema.

Nov 2007 – Gospel of Peace Church established in Glasgow by Yohanes and Eskider.

2007 – Christ Covenant Church established in Birmingham by Isayas Daniel.

Jul 2007 – First television broadcast – Elshaddai Amharic Christian TV – started by Abera and Beletu Habte.

June 2008 – Leeds Christian Fellowship Church established by group of Christians

2016 – Emmanuel Oromo Church Manchester established by group of Oromo Christian refugees.

Dec 2016 – Emmanuel Evangelical Church established in Glasgow by Ergate Ayana.